'Hindu', 'Hinduism' and such other related words are persian in origin, and are derived from the word 'Sindhu', the river. 'Sindhu' became 'Hindu' in Persian, and then the people living in the region of the Sindhu river were called the Hindus and their religion Hinduism. Hinduism represent the ancient most living religion and culture of the world. In ancient times Hinduism was called 'Brahmanism' or 'Vedantism'. It is also called the 'Sanatana Dharma'. 'Sanatana' means eternal and everlasting and 'Dharma' means something which upholds or maintains. Thus 'Sanatana Dharma' stands for the law which upholds and maintains life and order. It also underline the fact that Hinduism has neither a beginning nor an end. It is eternal and everlasting and its beginning cannot be fixed in terms of time and its originator.

HINDUISM

DR. B. R. KISHORE

DIAMOND POCKET BOOKS

ISBN 81-7182-603-2

© **Publisher**

Publisher	:	**DIAMOND POCKET BOOKS (P) LTD.**
		X-30, Okhla Industrial Area, Phase-II,
		New Delhi-110020
		Ph. : (011) 6841033, 6822803, 6822804
		Fax : (011) 6925020
E-mail	:	mverma@nde.vsnl.net.in
Website	:	www.diamondpocketbooks.com
Edition	:	2001
Price	:	Rs. 95/-
Price	:	US $ 7/-
Typesetting	:	**TIMES GRAPHICS**
		RZ-50/6, Tughlakabad Extn., New Delhi-44
		Ph. : 6077081
Printer	:	Adarsh Printers, Navin Shahdra, Delhi-32

PREFACE

The roots of Hinduism reach deep into pre-historic hoary past. It has evolved over these millennia, and still this process continues. Dynamism, tolerance, cattholicity, assimilation, inclusiveness, optimism and unity in diversity have always been its hallmarks. Its multiplicity is more apparent than real. In the ultimate analysis, Hinduism proves to be a great synthesis of many diverse and even conflicting and contradictory trends and elements. Thus, its multiplicity and ambivalence are not only incompatible with the concept of essential unity of life and its creator, but also mark its strength. The Vedas and Vedanta form the earliest source of our knowledge of Hinduism. The Vedanta literature reflects mainly the early ritual-side of the Hindu way of living. So do the Puranas, as they throw significant light on the various mundane aspects of later Hinduism. The two Epics and the Gita also delineate the basis tenets of Hinduism, and underline the desirability of dharma and righteous living, leading to ultimate triumph of the forces of good over evil.

The relization of Reality or Self, leading to final liberation, is one of the fundamentals of Hinduism. In this sense, yoga is efflorescence and fruition of Hinduism. Hinduism is not only a religion, but also a way of living and thinking. As such, its contribution towards world heritage and culture has been quite tremendous and unparalleled. Hinduism has exercised a great influence on world-minds in respect of abstract speculation, religion, arts and science. The well-known six systems of Hindu philosophy, are still a great force to be reckoned with. Thus, it has been a kindly light on the path of Pilgrim's Progress of humanity. One of the most characteristic qualities of Hinduism, is that it never believes in conversion, and there has never been a recognizable attempt at proselytization. There is no religious conquest on record. It has been a great living force in the life of millions of people on the subcontinent and in foreign lands.

In spite of its many drawbacks such as casteism, untouchability, superstitions, dogmas, and other ills, Hinduism is rational and scientific at its core. These shortcomings and ills may touch it, but they can never penetrate its spirit. In this sense, many of the ills of Hinduism can be said to be extraneous and peripheral. But they are to be condemned in no uncertain terms, and must be eliminated.

The present book is rather a fall out of my comprehensive readings in Hinduism over these years. I feel indebted indeed to many authors, especially for textual quotations. My attempt here has been to bring into focus the panormic view of the popular Hinduism as well as its abiding and eternal principles, in a style simple and direct and yet lucid and vigorous.

—Dr. B. R. KISHORE

CONTENTS

Lord Shri Ganeshji

Lord Ganesh — considered as first amongst gods and being the
remover of obstacles and is also known as Vighneshvara.

CHAPTER ONE

Hinduism : History and Heritage

'Hinduism' is a modern term, but it represents the ancient most living religion and culture of the world. In ancient times Hinduism was called 'Brahmanism' or 'Vedantism'. It is also called the 'Sanatana Dharma'. 'Sanatana' means eternal and everlasting, and 'Dharma' means something which upholds or maintains. Thus 'Sanatana Dharma' stands for the law which upholds and maintains life and order. It also underline the fact that Hinduism has neither a beginning nor an end. It is eternal and everlasting and its beginning cannot be fixed in terms of time and its originator. Like Christianity and Islam, Hinduism does not owe its origin to one prophet or a religious book. It has evolved through these epochs and ages and still continues to grow. There is no single human agency or personality at the root of Hinduism. Hinduism is the religion of the majority in India, and over 80% of the Indian population are the Hindus. It is eternal and everlasting in this sense also that it has escaped the fate that overtook the religion of Egypt, Mesopotamia and Babylonia of ancient times.

'Hindu', 'Hinduism' and such other related words are Persian in origin, and are derived from the word 'Sindhu', the river. 'Sindhu' became 'Hindu' in Persian, and then the people living in the region of the Sindhu river were called the Hindus and their religion Hinduism. The terms 'Hindu' and 'Hinduism' were later extended to the people of the whole sub-continent and their way of living and thinking. In the beginning the extent of the people and their civilization were actually far more widespread than the expanse indicated by such words as Hindu and Hinduism. In Greek Sindhu became 'Indus', and from it were derived India and Indian. Thus 'Indian' is an anglicised word meaning the 'land of Indus'. Hindu now cannotes the whole spread of religious, cultural and philosophical way of thinking and living of the entire sub-continent.

The word 'Hinduism' is geographical in origin, and geography has played a very vital role in the growth and formulation of the thinking and practices of the Hindus. Obviously, Hinduism is a product of the interplay of the forces of Indian geography and ancient Indian genius. India's geographical features have considerable influenced, both directly and indirectly, her religion and way of living. India is a vast country, a sub-continent with her fantastic and formidable an arc of the Himalayas in the extreme north, and the vast sea round her southern peninsular plateau. India's great latitudinal spread, encompassing a wide range of climates and temperatures, made it rich for the advent and development of a great and multi-dimensional religion such as Hinduism and its off-shoots like Buddhism, Jainism and Sikhism.

The vast plains of the Sindhu and the Ganga, one of greatest stretches of the flat alluvial areas of our planet, were the cradle-ground of early Hindu religion and culture. The great size, the splendid isolation, the protection provided by the mighty Himalayas and the seas, the rich and fertile alluvial soil, abundant rain and the generous bounty of nature made India a fit ground for intellectual pursuit, philosophical speculations and abstract thinking. It is India's characteristic geographical features, which have imbued the Indian wisdom with great maturity and matchless mellowness. In spite of numerous geographical regions, different climates, etc., India has been culturally and religiously one and unified. Hinduism, as a religion and cultural force, has been a great unifying single force in India. Amidst diversity of rituals and customs, there can be seen a certain uniformity and similarity at higher religious and intellectual levels. It were India's mountains, rivers, forests and sea-shores that exercised an abiding influence on Hindu speculation and way of life. For a Hindu they all have a deep divinity about them, and so they are worshipped and deified. The Himalayas have been the abode of the Hindu gods and goddesses. It is on the banks and confluences of the rivers that many Hindu pilgrimage centres are located. It was in the sylvan forests that the Hindu tapovans, retreats, hermitages and gurukulas were situated, where the aspirants, rishis and students practised austerities, tapas and learning. It was her in the forest retreats that Upanishads were born and developed.

10

It is the religious thinking and affinity, coupled with moral values and abstract thinking, which cuts across all geographical and political barriers. In spite of diverse ritual practices, attitudes and thinking, a single ideology prevails at a deeper level. It is again the bounty of nature that helped considerably in making the Hindus so tolerant, catholic, non-violent and generally vegetarian. They developed a sense of affection, bordering veneration to the cow in particular and other animals and birds in general. Consequently many birds and animals came to be associated with Hindu deities, and they became their vehicles and mounts.

Nature had destined India to develop her religion in a splendid isolation and yet there is no other land that has had such a rich and varied intercourse with so different peoples, religions, cultures and thinking. Geographically isolated, but historically it has been a great meeting point of various cultures and civilizations all these centuries. India and its religion(s) have outlived the test of time and invasions. Empires have risen and fallen, kings have come and gone like bubbles, but India with her vibrant culture and Sanatana Dharma continues to march forward triumphantly. Diversity and assimilation have always been the hall-mark of this eternal land. Many races and conquerors came, but they all lost their individualities in this marvel of the Indian melting pot.

Hinduism represents a succession of rich cultural epochs. Since its beginning in dim and hoary pre-historical past, its flow has been steadily maintained with interruption. It is very comprehensive and inclusive religion, but its diversity is not incompatible with its underlying essential unity. It represents a formidable synthesis of numerous elements, all fused together into a great organic whole. Hinduism, in fact, is a rainbow coloured fabric and a symphonious way of life. This immense synthesis and symphony has been the result of ceaseless efforts of Indian wisdom since days dating back to five-six millennia. It is a composite religion, a veritable ocean to which many rivers and streams of religions, races and cultures have meaningfully contributed in their own way. The diversity of its creeds, dogmas, rituals, images and idols is simply external and instrumental. Its many facetedness does not mean that Hinduism is an amalgam of diverse religions, faiths and attitudes. The spiritual growth and evolution involves many stages from the lower forms of worship to the higher ones, and hence it allows the soul to evolve in full freedom according to its capacity and inclination. It does not believe in uniformity, regimentation or conversion.

for they would defeat the very purpose of the religion.

The Hindus are the lineal descendants of the famous ancient Aryan race. In the beginning the Aryans were confined to the Sapta-sindhu region between the rivers Sindhu or Indus and the Sarasvati, now lost. This region was then called 'Brahmavarta' or 'Aryavarta'. Gradually the Aryans spread out to the Gangetic plain and the regions further east and south of the country. By the time Aryanization and Aryan settlement in the south were almost complete, the country came to be known as 'Bharata' or 'Bharatavarsha', after the great Bharatas, whose descendants fought a terrible battle among themselves known as Mahabharata. Even today the country is called by its traditional name 'Bharata'.

The Aryans came from out of India, and with that began a new epoch and a transition from the Mohen-jo-daro, Harappan urban civilization to a predominently rural and pastoral way of living and speculation. The Aryans were possessed of refined poetic sensibilities and were far more advanced in the use of metals, economy, industry and means of transportation. They were vigorous and a fighting race, and had no difficulty in assimilating partly the Indus-Valley civilization and religion.

The fact that Indus Valley civilization and religion are closely related to Hinduism have been amply borne out by the terracotta figurines, seals etc., found there in the excavations. The practice of penance, yoga, worship of Shiva or Pashupati and Mother Goddess as deities of fertility were part and parcel of Harappan religion. They were later incorporated into Hinduism. The iconic and phallic worship, pre-eminence of Mother Goddess Durga or Kali, ascetic and yogic practices of Hinduism can be directly traced to Harappan religion, which was essentially pre-Vedic and non-Aryan. The Aryans were definitely more vigorous and a fighting race. They possessed fine horses, chariots, and arrows of iron. They were superior to the Harappan people, but religiously and culturally the Harappans were better placed than the Aryans. And so the Aryans incorporated into their religion a lot of already existing Indian religion and culture. Therefore, Aryan religion and culture did not in any way imply the regression in the scale of progression but rather it marked an advancement, synthesis and assimilation of already existing cult into the exuburant and ever-growing Hinduism. The discovery of the Indus Valley civilization has pushed the history of Indian religions and culture as far

12

back as 3500 B.C. Thus in Harappan religion can be seen the ancestor of Hinduism. How did this wonderful religion and culture came to an end? Perhaps the successive waves of the Aryan invasion caused it, but the invaders wisely imbibed and assimilated many religious elements of the conquered. The recurrent images of Proto-Shiva with exposed phallus, the Bull and statutes of nude female, with a plant issuing forth from the womb, do anticipate many predominant features of the early Brahmanism and later Hinduism.

The earliest source of our knowledge of Hinduism are Vedas and the Upanishads. These are the ancient most monuments of Hindu culture and religion. They form the rock foundations of the magnificent edifice of Hinduism, and also of its off-shoots and extensions like Buddhism and Jainism. The Vedas are a whole body of literature and their parts represent successive stages in the evolution of Hinduism. The exact time of their composition is difficult to trace out. The earlier limit of the Vedas is placed somewhere between 2000 and 2500 B.C. The Vedic literature was handed down orally from one generation to another till it was written down sometime one millennium B.C. the Rigveda is the oldest of the Vedas. The three more Vedas were composed during the later Vedic period. These are Yajur, Sama and Atharva Vedas. All these great and ancient religious books of the Hindus consist of three parts, that is, Samhitas, Brahmanas and Aranyakas. Samhitas are the collection of sacred hymns in verse and belong to the earliest stage. They are addressed to various male and female deities. The Brahmana portions are mostly in prose and describe in detail the rites and rituals. The Aranyakas (forests treatises are in a sense supplements and continuation of the Brahmanas. These three parts form the Vedas proper. The Upanishads or the Vedant, which mark the culmination of the abstract speculation and contain the richest philosophical and religious teachings, are mostly parts of the Aranyakas or the Forest Treatises. Many Aranyakas are now lost, and only the Upanishadic portions of these profoundly philosophical books have escaped the erosion and ravages of time. There are many Upanishads, but the principal ones are sixteen or so in number. This whole literature contains deep spiritual truths and philosophy. The central teaching of the Upanishads underline the identity of the Supreme Soul and the individual Soul. "Tatt-twam-asi" (That thou art!) can be said the quintessence of Vedant and Hinduism. That stands for Brahman, the Supreme and Universal Soul or the Cosmic Purusha.

Then comes Vedangas or Sutra literature consisting of such works as Kalpasutras, the Grihyasutras and the Srautasutras. This literature deals with supplementary sciences or the lower knowledge. These books describe in detail the rules of ceremonies, sacrifices and such rites as belong to conception, birth, wedding, funeral, initiation and other customs, usages and rituals of Hindu domestic life. This literature is important for the interpretation of the Vedas as it contains the rules regarding the use of various mantras, hymns, prayers and incantations.

The Vedic literature is isoteric and contains spiritual truths, not fully expressed but implicitly revealed, the Sutra literature and Puranas are essentially exoteric and deal with external social and domestic conduct and rituals. So are two national epics, the Ramayana and the Mahabharata. The Ramayana is the epic poem composed by the sage and Adi Kavi Valmiki. It deals with the adventures and exploits of hero Rama. Rama, the incarnation of Vishnu, upholds Dharma and Maintains righteousness by his most noble deeds and exemplary actions. Rama, the embodiment of Hindu excellence is held in the highest honour and the worship paid to him, his consort Sita and devotee monkey-god Hanuman, the epitome of selfless service, devotion, faithfulness, obedience and manly strength, is of the purest nature. Another great Hindu epic, the Mahabharata's authorship is attributed to Krishna Dwaipayana or Vyasa. It relates the great war fought among the Bharatas, and is the longest epic poem in the world. The Kauravas and the Pandavas, the descendants of the Bharatas through Puru of the Lunar dynasty, fought a terrible war for the kingdom of Hastinapur. The most important part of the Mahabharata is the portion in which Krishna the manifestation of the highest divinity, expounds to Arjuna the most profound truth of Vedanta and Yoga in the form of a dialogue called the Bhagavad Gita. The Gita or the Song Celestial is one of the greatest philosophical works which has exercised a powerful influence on the Hindus for the last many centuries. The Mahabharata is later than the Ramayana, but it is not possible to give the dates of composition of these two great epics, though the question of exact chronology has troubled the minds of the scholars for long.

The Puranas are the later sacred literature of the Hindus. The principal Puranas are 18, but it is difficult to give their exact chronology or their date of composition. Many of them certainly existed before the coming of Gautam Buddha, but some of them are of the later period. They are rooted in the Vedas and represent a later and more elaborate development of Hinduism. The Puranas deal with powers and deeds of the gods, heroes, saints and ancestors of the human race. Didactic in spirit, they are dedicated to some god or the other and his cult. They were chiefly meant for the common people, who had no access to, and understanding to the abstract speculations of the Vedas and the Vedanta. Thus, the Puranas as sacred scriptures can be considered as the books of second grade. The Puranas are valuable in the sense that they throw a great deal of light on various aspects of Hinduism. The Puranas served the purpose of educating the masses and the unlettered Hindus through their tales, legends, mythology, rituals, theism and pantheism. The Puranas are in verse and their form is always that of a dialogue between an exponent and an enquirer or aspirant, interspersed with the comments and observations of other people. Of the Puranas, the Bhagavata Purana is the most popular among the Hindus. It is called Bhagvata because it is dedicated to Bhagvata or Vishnu. In its tenth book is related in detail the life of Krishna, the manifestation of Vishnu. The Puranas as scriptures are the great authorities of Hinduism and have considerable influence on Hindu thinking and religious practices. The two great epics, mentioned earlier, also partake of the character of the Puranas. The Ramayana, the Mahabharata and the Bhagavata Purana are still read and recited with great delight and interest during certain months of the year among the Hindus. Puranas are pluralistic and sectarian in their approach, yet they never completely lose sight of the monatheistic conception of God or Reality.

Yoga 'the science of the soul', a sure means of spiritual discipline and the realization of the reality, is one of the fundamental of the Hinduism. As one of the Shaddarshanas or the six schools of philosophy, it was founded by rishi Patanjali. The Yoga Sutras of Patanjali, is well known all over the world. This school emphasizes the practice of meditation as a chief means of final liberation. In a broad sense, yoga is an integral part of all Hindu systems and practices. The need for yogic discipline is also underlined in the Upanishads. Yoga makes the whole being of the aspirant ready to be in direct touch with the cosmic consciousness. Yoga quickens spiritual evoultion by making a yogi's nature refined, disciplined and more rhythmical. As a psychic discipline and training, yoga makes individual's life richer by revealing the subtler and finer aspects of the individual's consciousness.

The other schools or systems of Shad-darshanas include the Nyaya philosophy of Gautama, the Vaisheshika school of Kanada, the Sankhya system of the sage Kapila, the Purva Mimansa of Jaimini and the Uttara Mimansa or the Vedanta philosophy. All these systems have the one and the same goal, the final liberation of the soul and its absorption into the Supreme Soul, but the paths are different. The Nyaya system is based on reasoning, analysis and dialectics and therefore, it is also called the Logical School. And Gautama is also called the Aristotle of India. The Hindu syllogism consists of Proposition, Reason, Instance, Application of the Reason, and the Conclusion. This school underlines the necessity of clear and logical thinking as a means of final release and moksha. It is exoteric in its approach and combines both deductive and inductive methods of reasoning, for example:-

1. Whatever has smoke has fire, e.g., the kitchen.

2. This hill is smoky.

3. Smoke is always accompanied by fire.

4. It is the nature of fire to create smoke.

5. Therefore, this hill is fiery (is volcanic).

Thus, the Hindus were the first to invent logic and reasoning. Vaisheshika of Kanada is supplementary to the Nyaya, and these two schools are classed together as the Nyaya-Vaisheshika. Vaisheshika system traces the origin of the universe to eternal atoms, and so it is also called the Atomic School.

The Sankhya and the Yoga systems have much in common, and therefore they are classed together, but the former is atheistical and the latter theistical. It is based on the fundamental duality of Purusha and Prakriti, or the spirit and the matter. Purusha manifests himself through this Prakriti. Prakriti is endowed with the three gunas, the Sattava, the Rajas and the Tamas. The dualism of Purusha and Prakriti, or the soul and matter and the atheism of the Sankhya were modified to suit the later popular Hinduism and its manifestations in montheism and pantheism.

The Purva Mimansa of Jaimini and Uttara Mimansa of Vyasa are classed together. The latter is subdivided into Dvaita, Vishishtadvaita and Advaita schools. "The object of both these schools is to teach the art of reasoning with the express purpose of aiding the interpretation of the Vedas, not only in the speculative but the practical portion". Purva Mimansa which literally means previous investigation or enquiry, deals with rites, rituals, ceremonies and all that is formal, instrumental and external of Hindu religious practice. The Uttara Mimansa or Vedanta's principal tenets are that " God is the omniscient and omnipotent cause of the existence, continuance and dissolution of the universe. Creation is an act of his will; he is both the efficient and the material cause of the world......God is the sole-existent and universal soul, he is adwaita, with out a second". The three sub-schools of the Vedanta are three successive steps of the same philosophy. They all underline the existence of Brahman as the basis of all manifestations, which is absolute existence (Sat), intelligence or consciousness (Chit) and bliss (Ananda). Vedanta is the most important of the six systems and forms the hub of modern Hinduism. The Brahma Sutras is the principal text of this school of philosophy. Adi Shankracharya was the great exponent of this school.

The six Vadangas or the Limbs of the Vedas deal with subsidiary sciences. They consists of (i) Kalpa or religious performances, (ii) Siksha or the science of phonetics and pronunciation, (iii) Chhandas or metre and prosody, (iv) Nirukta or etymology, (v) Vyakarna or grammar, and (vi) Jyotish or astronomy and astrology. The Upa-Vedas dealt with Ayurveda or medical science, Dhamurveda or the military science, Gandharvaveda or the science of music and Arthashastra or the science of wealth and polity.

The all-pervasive and inclusive Hinduism developed and continues to grow within this broad speculative religious framework. Hinduism is not only the oldest living religion, but it is also one of the noblest way and view of life. It has faced many challenges and still there are many at present. But it has taken all such challenges into its strides as an ever evolving and dynamic religion. It has changed in response to the demands of the changing times without ever violating the fundamental principles and their continuity. In modern times Hinduism found its fullest expression in the life and works of such great men as Rama, Krishna, Paramhansa, Vivekanand, Dayanand Saraswati and Mahatma Gandhi!. Gandhi was a devout and true Hindu. Underlining its strength and also its weak points, he once said, "I can no more describe my feeling for hinduism than for my wife. She moves me as no other woman in the world can. Not that she has no faults; I dare say she has many more than I see, myself. But the feeling of an indissoluble bond is there. Even so I feel for and about Hinduism with all its faults and limitations....I am a reformer through and through. But my zeal never takes me the rejection of any of the essential things of Hinduism ....Hinduism is not an exclusive religion. In it there is room for the worship of all the prophets of the world. It is not a missionary religion in the ordinary sense of the term.....Hinduism tells everyone to worship God according to his own faith or Dharma, and so it lives at the peace with all the religions".

Tolerance and assimilation are the hallmarks of Hinduism. The ethnic invasions of the Persians, Greeks. Kushanas, Hunas and others continued unabated for centuries, but ultimately they all lost their individual identities in the melting point of Hinduism and Indian culture and became one with it. The Hindus incorporated so many elements into their culture from these races and ethnic groups, but they so imbibed and assimilated these elements that they became their own. The process of Hinduization has been quite subtle, continuous and long. The impact of the alien influences could create the ripples and wavelets on the upper surface of the Hinduism, but its inner waters always remained calm and yet respective. These wonderous powers of assimilation and absorption have been operating since the dawn of civilization in this subcontinent. Its respectivity and powers of digestion and adaptation strikes one with wonder. In the past it assimilated the various cultural and religious elements and still it continues doing so the western influences. With each new contact, whether it was with the Greeks, Romans, Scythians, Arabs, Persians or the Christians, it grew richer in experience and excellence. Every successive reciprocation in speculation and culture enriched Hinduism.

At times Hinduism degenerated into dogmas, superstitions, social and religious evils like casteism, untouchability, child-marriage, infanticide, sati-pratha, and score others, and it was beset with stagnation, but then there appeared great souls and heroes who rejuvenated by purging it of superstitious, evil practices and the dead wood of stereotyped customs and traditions. For example, in the medieavel times there appeared on the scene such great socio-religious reformers as Ramanuja (1050-1151), Ramananda (15th century A.D.), Kabirs, (1440-1518), Nanak (1469-1533), Tukaram, Chaitanya Mahaprabhu and others who revived the eternal Hindu ideals of brotherhood tolerance, essential unity of all life, equality before God and such other human and cultural values. They condemned in no uncertain terms the evils of casteism, sati, infanticide, drinking, child-marriage, and superstitions. They provided Hinduism with much needed re-orientation and stressed the oneness of God, though his names are legion. In modern times this revival, rehabilitation and regeneration was affected by Raja Ram Mohan roy (1772-1833), Rama Krishna Paramhansa (1833-1886), Dayanand Sarasvati (1824-1883) and Mahatma Gandhi (1869-1948).

The Hindu hospitality too and tolerance of alien faiths and religions is well-known. One of the basic teachings of Hinduism is that all paths lead to God, and various religions and faiths are these paths. The jews have been living in India well over 2000 years in peace, freedom and perfect equality. First of all they settled in Kerala and Cochin. When they came to India, they were allowed not only to practice their religion in full freedom, but were also granted rich largess of land and money to built their synagogues. The jews in India are mainly confined to Cochin, Pune, Bombay and Delhi. In Cochin they have a magnificent synagogue built in 1568. They fled the land of their origin jerusalem to escape the religious persecution and migrated to the tolerant and hospitable Hindu climate of India.

Similarly, the Parsis or Zoroastrians came to India in the early 8th century seeking refuge from religious persecution in Iran. The first batches of Parsi pilgrims settled in Delhi and Gujarat and then on west coast of India in Maharashtra. The Parsis, the followers of Zaruthustra, are an enterprising community and have done a great deal for the development and growth of the country's industry, commerce and finance.

The Christian church in South India is much older than Islam. St. Thomas, one of the first twelve disciples of Christ, was the preacher of Christianity in India. Soon after Jesus's crucifixion, he arrived in India, and began his missionary work. He was contemporary of St. Peter in Rome. But it was much later that Christian Missions came to India and converted many Indians, mainly low caste Hindus. The spread of Islam began in India with the Muslim conquests in the country, but Arab contacts with India go long back before the coming of the prophet Mohammad. There were some Muslim settlements along the west coast of penisular India before the coming of Islam in India in a big way. Today India is one of the largest Islamic nations. Thus, in India there never has been any religious persecution or intolerance. In recent times there have been some communal riots and disturbances, but they owe their birth to certain political vested interests and such other factors, and Hinduism has nothing to do with these; Hinduism has never been a militant and violent religion. Its actual strength lies in its vast powers of tolerance, absorption, assimilation, even of conflicting points, and resilience. That is why Hinduism has survived the ravages and corrosion of time. It is a religion of reconciliation, harmony and concord.

The immance of God in every living being is fundamental to Hinduism. Every animate thing is sacred and important, let alone a human being. Therfore, there is no room for intolerance or fanaticism on any ground. Hinduism is the path of peace, and it resides in harmony.

The Hindu contribution towards world heritage and culture has been great and matchless. Hinduism has exercised a great influence in the fields of abstract thought. religion, arts and science on the western minds. Hindu influence on ancient Greek culture and early Christianity is an established fact. The Hindu Shada-darshana or six system of philosophy are still a great force to be reckoned. In the words of Mrs. Annie Besant, "They remain as monuments of pure intellection. Remarkable not only for the perfection with which the reasoning is conducted, but also for the training they gave to the human mind; the nature of the things is sought into, and in order that error may be avoided there is the keenest analysis of the tools by which that investigation is to be made". In the words of Sir Monier Williams, a great scholar and Indologist, "The Hindus were Spinozaites more than

20

two thousand years before the existence of Spinoza; and Darwinians many centuries before our time, and before any word like 'evolution' existed in any language of the world". Many modern thinkers of the West like Goethe, Hegel, Schopenhauer, Emerson, Threau, T.S. Eliot, W.B. Yeats, Walt Whitman, Richard Jeffries, Edward Carpenter have admitted their indebtedness to Hindu-thought and speculation. Hinduism has been a leading light on the path of pilgrim's Progress of Humanity.

CHAPTER TWO

The Vedas and the Upanishads

What is known under the generic name of the Vedas are the ancient most monuments of the Hindu religiophilosophic thought. They are also the oldest human documents. By dint of their profound wisdom, they could escape the ravages of time. They have withstood the acid test of time all these centuries, and today form an important part of the common heritage of mankind. They are a whole body of literature, and the earliest source of our knowledge about Hindu view and way of life. They are called "Srutis" revelations, orally transmitted to the seers by God himself. They were not composed or written down by the ancient seers and rishis. The Vedas are considered "Apaurusheya", that is, their authorship cannot be assigned to any prophet or human agency. They were breathed out by God and heard and envisioned by the ancient sages in the dim and pre-historic past in india. Thus, they are impersonal spiritual knowledge, and wisdom received by the seers. They were not their authors individually or collectively, but were blessed with the divine inner audience from him. They received this esoteric knowledge of the Vedas in a state of mind which can be termed as a state of supra-normal consciousness. This non-authorship of the Vedas imparts them a peculiar universality of their own. Their being non-personal in a composition also means that in sense anybody who studies them, delves deep, and imbibes their spirit, is their author.

These ancient most books of the Hindu lore and learning are four in number. They are the Rigveda, the Samaveda, the Yajurveda and the Atharvaveda. But they are generally spoken of as a "trayi", the triple vidya or the threefold knowledge. It is because the last one, that is, the Atharvaveda is relatively of later date. Therefore, they are invariably referred to as the "Triple Eternal Vedas" (trayam brahm sanatanam). These four together form the foundation of Brahmanic or Hindu religion philosophic systems and schools.

22

Broadly speaking, the Vedas consist of three parts, viz., Samhitas, Brahmanas and Aranyakas. The Upanishads are also their part, but they are treated separately because of their high speculative contents. The Upanishads are also called the 'Vedanta'. The Samhita portion of the Vedas contains "mantras" of hymns and mark the earliest stage of the creation of the respective Vedas. A Samhita literally means a collection. They are a kind of sacred religious songs meant to be recited or sung in offering worship and sacrifice to various gods and goddesses. The Brahmanas, which are mostly in prose, describe how to perform various rites and rituals, and thus form together with the hymns, the books of karmakanda. The Brahmanas are actually the commentaries on the Samhitas. The Aranyakas, or the forest treatises deal with meditation, while the Upanishads deal with the highest spiritual knowledge. The Upanishads, which are in rhythmic prose, contain secret or esoteric knowledge of the supreme kind. The Upanishads, in fact, represent the florescence and fruition of the speculative philosophy and religious wisdom contained in the Vedas, and that is why they are also referred to as the Vedanta. In the Vedas the emphasis on rituals and prayer, and in the Upanishads the centre of gravity shifts on contemplation, Atmajnana or Self-knowledge, mysticism and morality. The word "Upanishad" literally signifies "setting at rest ignorance by revealing the knowledge of the Supreme Spirit". The Brahmanas interpret and comment upon the Samhita texts of the Vedas, while the Upanishads interpret their philosophy. Thus, they are all harmonius and homogeneous.

The Vedic literature is in Sanskrit. The Rigveda is the oldest and also the most important. The Rigveda Samhita contains 10,000 verses in the form of mantras or hymns. These hymns were orally transmitted from generation to generation in certain families for a considerable long period before they were written down, and in this process they were subjected to many changes. The Rigvedic hymns belong to Hotar priests and were sung at the time of sacrifices. Samaveda belongs to the Udgatr priests and is meant to be chanted at the time of sacrifice; the term 'saman' means a melody, and designates a whole Samhita of the Samaveda, because it is meterial. Except the 75 hymns found here, the rest are borrowed from the Rigveda. Of these 75 hymns, some are partly found in other Samhitas.

23

Yajurveda is the sacrificial prayer book of the Adhvaryu priests. It is composed in verse of different metres and also in prose. They represent the loftiest human sentiments that a man can ever feel for his god or goddess. Many of its mantras have been taken from the Rigveda. Yajurveda is characterized by its division into two collection of texts. The first is called Krishna or Black Yajurveda. The second is known as Shukla or White Yajurveda. In the former the Samhita and Brahmana portions are confused, but in the latter Brahmana portion is collected separately in the Satpatha Brahmana.

The Atharvaveda also shares many hymns in common with Rigveda. It is comparatively of later date, but its many hymns are as old as the Samhita mantras of the Rigveda. Atharvaveda will ever remain one of the richest human heritages representing both the secular and the intellectual aspects of the ancient Hinduism. The term "atharvan" was associated from the earliest times with intellectualism. Many of the hymns of Atharvaveda are highly speculative. The three earlier Vedas represent mainly the aspects of ancient Hinduism dealing with the goal of man's life to come, and the Atharvaveda deals with the other aspect, that is, the life of man in this world. This Veda deals with man, his daily life, his safety from the enemy, destruction of the foe, polities, cures, curses, atonements and such other things. But at the same time Atharvaveda is intimately and deeply concerned with the question of the Absolute.

The Upanishads are great scientific works on metaphysics and ethics. In the words of R.D. Ranade, "They mark the transition from the Nature-gods to Self, from the hymnology to reflection, from henotheistic polytheism to monotheistic mysticism. No longer is there any fear of the wrath of the personified gods; and so, they mark the transition from emotion and imagination of the Rigveda to thought and reason of the post-Vedic period. Hence, the guardian of natural and moral order does not come from without, but springs from the Atman who is the synthesis of what is both outside and inside and who is veritably the ballast of nature."

But it does not mean that Upanishads mark a departure from the Vedas. They have their roots in the Vedas. Here we find those ideas in well-developed forms which were in the form of the seeds in the Vedas. Thus, the Upanishads mark the natural and logical growth of the Vedic thoughts. They are several, but only sixteen of these are

24

recognised as authentic and authoritative. These are, Aitreya and Kaushitaki (Rigveda); Katha, Taittiriya, Kaivalya, Svetasvatra and Narayana (Black Yajurveda); Isa, Brihadaranyaka and Jabala (White Yajurveda). Prasna, Mundaka, Mandukya and Nrisimhatapani belong to Atharvaveda. The Upanishads belong to different periods of Indian history, and the earliest of these are pre-Buddhistic, and are believed to have been composed between 1000 B.C. and 300 B.C. The Upanishads are called the Vedanta, not only because they come at the end of Vedas, but also because they mark the culmination and consummation of them. The Upanishads presuppose the Vedas, and the latter anticipate the Upanishads.

THE ORIGINS

When and how did the universe began? Whence did this phenomenal world originate? By what do beings live and on what established? These were the profound questions which engaged the minds of the ancient Hindu sages and seers. The Hindu seers of old were the first to penetrate the mystery of creation. The Vedic literature is the first scientific and recorded attempt to explain the evolution of the universe and life. These ancient texts underline the restlessness and stirrings of the human mind to discern a certain meaning and essence of life and its relation with universe and its creator. The inner urge and the great driving force of the rishis made them explore the beginnings of the existence, when nothing existed, neither the sky, nor the earth, nor space in between, neither God nor gods, because then God was not yet God having created nothing. We find the Vedic rishi in Svetasvatra Upanishad enquire, "What is the cause? Brahman? Whence do we originate? By what do we live and on what established? Upheld by what in pleasure and in reverse live we our respective lives. O Brahman Knowers?" The same enquiry is repeated again and again in so many pleces. The Rigveda asks, "Who verily knows and who can here declare it, whence it was born and whence comes this creation? The gods are later than this world's production, who knows then whence it came first into being?" And then doubtfully answers, "He, the first origin of this creation, whether he formed it all or did not form it, whose eye controls this world in highest heaven, he verily knows it, or perhaps he knows not".

The universe must have a beginning. In the beginning naught

existed. It was all darkness enveloped in darkness, far and wide, nothing but absolute void, until one out of the void took birth, he became self aware and felt alone, and so desired to be many, wanted himself to be multiplied. He reflected and having reflected, he projected it, he entered into it, that very thing, and became the gross and the subtle. The Prasnopanishad explains the beginning of the evolution thus-

"The Pursha then first of all created Prana; for, Prana it is who is the inner Self of all the beings in the universe and the very support of the organs of sense and action of them all. He then produced the five elements as the material out of which the body was formed. First he produced the element for space (akasha) with its specific quality of sound; then out of akasha the wind, with its specific quality of touch in addition to the quality of sound, because of its being a product of; then out of wind, the element of fire with the specific quality of form and along with it the inherited qualities of sound and touch; then again, out of fire the element of water with its specific quality of flavour, along with the three earlier qualities of sound, touch and form; and finally out of water, the element of earth and its specific quality of smell, along with the four qualities of the preceding elements, namely sound, touch, form and flour. And further, again, in order to make possible the acquistion of knowledge, and the doing of actions. He brought into being out of the elements and their qualities, the five senses of knowledge, as also the five organs of action. And in order that all this should be owned and possessed by a master, as if, he produced the inner sense or the mind."

This riddle of creation is again answered by means of the sacrifice of Purusha. The Rigveda explains that, "all creatures are one-fourth of him, three-fourths of eternal life in heaven. With three-fourths Purusha went up : one fourth of him again was here. Then he strode out of every side over what eats not and what eats. When gods prepared the sacrifice with Purusha as their offering. Its oil was spring, the holy gift was autumn; summer was the wood. They blamed as victim on the grass Purusha born in earlier time. With him the Deities and all Sadhyas and Rishis sacrificed. From that great general sacrifice the dripping fat was gathered up. He formed the creatures of the air and animals both wild and tame. From it were horses born, from it all cattle with two rows of teeth. The Moon was gendered from his mind, and from his eye the Sun had birth, Indra and Agni from his mouth were born and Vayu from his breath. From his navel came mid air; the sky was fashioned from his head; Earth from his feet, and from his ear the regions. Thus they formed the worlds."

This cosmological question of creaion, one of the most philosophical ones, comes to the foreground again and again, and the creator is named as Prajapati or Brahmanaspati, Vishvakarman or Hiranyagarbha or gods in general, but it is emphasized again and again that all plurality is apparent not real. The reality is on, but is called by many names by the sages. When the question "What God shall we adore with our oblation?" is raised repeatedly, the answer is one alone, the Creator Prajapati, who holdeth up this heaven and earth, whose commandments all the gods acknowledge, the lord of the whole world of that breathes and slumbers, the God of gods, the universal germ.

The problem of creation and evolution occurs in the Brahmanas, in the Upanishads and again in the Gita and the Puranas, for example, in the Satpatha Brahmana we find that in the beginning Prajapati tortured and mortified himself in penance and created beings, and men out of his mind. Because men was created out of his mind, and mind being the most vital organ, man is the first and foremost of the beings. In other creation-legends the existence begins with primeval water or with the Brahman. Brahman is the ultimate cause of creation. From him all things are born, through him they live and finally into him they return and merge in. He is one without second and integral to the world of phenomena. From him the universe has come forth as threads from the spider. Thus, Vedic rishis were concerned not only with evolution but also with involution. In this respect these rishis are still ahead of the modern scientists. The involution or dissolution of the universe is in the inverse order. In dissolution each succeeding elements dissolve into its cause. Ultimately the universe is dissolved in the Purusha himself. And just as the rivers which run into the sea lose their names and forms and there remains one sea only, even so all things have no other destination except the Purusha, the only one omniscient Being in whom they all merge and lose their names and forms. What then remains is the eternal, immortal, timeless, Purusha, the Brahman. The universe has emanated from Brahman, a positive entity and ultimately returns to him. Herein we have the genesis of the theory of evolution and involution.

The Mundakya Upanishad declares that "As a spider projects and withdraws its web, as herbs grow on earth or hair comes on a living person, so does this universe here proceed from the immutable". The creation and dissolution of the universe is an eternal lila, a play of the Brahman. When we speak of the beginning of the universe, we actually speak of the beginning of a cycle (Kalpa). In this sense the Vedas declare the origin of the universe beginningless, because its origin cannot be traced.

Again in Kathopanishad this process of creation and dissolution is described beautifully. The Lord of Death, Yama tells Nachiketa, a great seeker of the truth, "Wonderful is this tree of wordly existence which has its roots upwards in the form of Brahman, and which, though it might not last even till the dawn of tommorrow and is therefore, known as the 'Asvatha' (not tomorrow lasting, and which also means the Pippala tree). The root being verily the Brahman, is the support and the sustenance of all the worlds. None can ever transgress its command."

"It comes out of Brahman, in it, it is sustained and in Brahman again it is dissolved. It is due to the fear of the Brahman that all the activities in the universe are going on smoothly, and without there being any exception or delay of even a single minute. It is through the fear of Brahman that fire burns, the sun shines, Indra rules over the gods, and wind and the Lord of Death are in great haste to perform their respective duties."

"He is within all beings and without-
Motionless, yet still moving, not discerned
For subtlety of instant presence; close
To all, to each; yet measurelessly far;
Not manifold, and yet subsisting still
In all which lives.
The light of lights, he is in the heart of dark
Shining eternally."

This process of creation and dissolution or pralaya goes on ceaselessly. Evolution and involution occur alternately as part of the lila of the Brahman. In Atharvaveda, Brahman as a Cosmic Pillar or Skambha is described as the source and support of all creation. It is this Cosmic Pillar which holds all things together. It is the source from which spring both being and non-being. The repeated query of this mantra, is, "What is Skambha? From which of his parts do the Fire, the Wind, the Moon, the Sun, the Earth and the Sky come forth? What is that Support which sustains the days, night, the world and all the forms of life? And how much of himself is there in the Skambha? By how mauch of himself did enter the Support? By how much will he into the future? That one limb he made thousand-fold, by how much of himself did he ᴇnter the Skambha? On whom the earth, the sky ᴀnd the air are firmly set, on whom the fire, the moon, the sun and the wind are firmly founded, each knowing his place? Tell me of that Skambha-who for sooth is he? In whose one limb all the thirty-three gods are set together, tell me of that Skambha, who may he be?"

And then, in reply the sages say that they who know this divine Purusha, know the Supreme Being, the Lord of life, the Support and frame of all creation, him, out of whose body were created the verses, formulae from his shavings, songs from his hairs. He alone holds the Adityas, Rudras, Vasus, and the rest of the three and thirty gods together, whose eyes are the sun and the moon, mouth the fire, breath the wind. "A great wonder amidst creation strode in penance on the surface of the sea. In him are set whatever gods there are, like the branches of a tree round the trunk. Unto him the gods continually render tribuite unmeasured in a well-measured place of sacrifice with their hands and feet, speech with hearing and with sight. He who knows the Reed of gold standing in the sea, is truly the mysterious Prajapati."

This theme of creation and dissolution recur in the Gita and the Puranas in great detail as the Brahman's eternal lila. In the Gita the same basic principles of evoultion underline the process of creation. It is He who manifests himself in and through the whole of the universe, each being reflecting a portion of his splendour. He is the beginning and the end, and also the in-between, "I am the origin of all; from me all things evolve. The wise know this and adore Me with all their heart..........I am the Self, O Gudakesa, seated in the hearts of all beings. I am the beiginning, the middle and also the end of all beings......whatever being there is, know that to have sprung from a spark of My splendour. I stand supporting the whole universe with a single fragment of Myself."

BRAHMAN AND ATMAN

The question of Brahman or ultimate Reality, and its relation to Atman or individual Soul, is fundamental to Hindu religious thinking. Brahman of the Hindus is both the personal God and the impersonal Reality, and they are not incompatible. This view of God, in both his aspects, underlines the principle of "from the familiar to the unfamiliar and from concreate to abstract". It represents a sublime synthesis of personal and impersonal, gross and subtle, microcasm and macrocasm, saguna and nirguna. The paths to the transcendental Reality pass through many stages. Paths may be different, but they all converge on the same one point of Reality.

Brahman is both immanent and transcendant. that is why he has been described in opposing terms and contradictory language. Brahman, in his saguna aspect, as a personal Deity, is the lord of all, omniscient, the cause of all. From him all beings originate and ultimately in him they merge. He is the ruler of the universe; he projects it, maintains it, and dissolves it at the end of the cosmic cycle. As Ishvara, he is the sum total of all the bodies in the universe, and the aggregate of all the minds. In the Rigveda, as Aditi, the boundless, infinite and indivisible, she is mother of all the gods. God is imagined here as one, immanent, indivisible Reality, the proginitor of the gods and the phenomenal world, "Aditi is the heaven, Aditi is mid-air, Aditi is the mother and the Sire and Son. Aditi is all gods, Aditi is five-classed men, Aditi is all that been born and shall be born."

The cosmic view of Reality holds God as saguna, the bearer of attributes. In the Purusha-Shukta of the Rigveda, he is described as having a thousand heads, a thousand eyes and a thousand feet and pervading the entire universe. It declares that all beings are only a fourth of the Reality and that God and man are inseparable, and the Supreme spirit as a Purusha or Cosmic Man involves inter-relationship.

"A thousand heads hath Purusha,

a thousand eyes, a thousand feet.

One every side pervading earth

He fills a space ten fingers wide.

This Purusha is all that yet hath been

and all that is to be;

the Lord of immortality which
Waxes greater still by food.
So mighty is his greatness;
Yea, greater than this is Purusha.
All creatures are one-fourth of him,
three-fourths eternal life in heaven.
With three-fourths Purusha went up,
one-fourth of him again was here.
Thence he strode out every side
over what eats not and what eats."

In the Upanishads he is both personal (saguna) and impersonal (nirguna). He is within and without, moving and unmoving. He is the ultimate Reality and cannot be described even by pairs of opposites. The Vedic bards are compelled to describe it in a dual manner. Brahma is the sole Reality, and yet there is a place for multitude of gods, goddesses and the phenomenal world as its manifestation. The theory of immanence holds God and the universe identical. The individual soul and the Supreme Soul are also identical in essence. Brahman is the foundation of all the manifestation. By knowing Brahman one becomes Brahman. The diversity of the phenomenal world and its identity with the Absolute is declared at many places in the Upanishads. From him has this universe come and to him it will return. He created it out of himself and then entered it. But this "entrance" is not to be taken literally. He does not enter like a builder, who builds a house and then enters it. He is there in all the living beings and yet he is one and undivided, immanent, all-pervasive and yet transcendent.

Brahman is the cause of all this manifestation. Just as gold can be shaped into various forms without any change into its fundamental nature, even so, Reality can manifest itself in diverse shapes and forms of various splendour and grandeur and yet remain the same. The different manifestation of the Divine are real but they cannot exist without the prior existence of That. In the words of Mundakopanishad, "Brahman has caused the show of the creation of the vast universe, which is very helpful to have some idea of the limitless magnitude, glory and the resplendent nature of the transcendent, uncontaminated, and impersonal Being. Fire is the form of him; heaven is his head; the

31

sun and the moon are his eyes; the quarters his ears; the Vedas his speech; the wind his prana; the whole world his heart; and the earth his feet, He is the infinite God, known as Vishnu, the inner Atman of all beings. From him is born the Sun, who is merely burning fuel in that great Fire; from him come forth the rains which produce herbs, and corn and valour in men and women from whom are born the various peoples". Brahman is Sat, Chit and Ananda, that is, He is absolute existence or being, absolute consciousness and absolute bliss.

Brahman being the sole Reality, the plurality of the world is unreal, and the result of avidya, maya or nescience. It is this nescience which is at the root of the experience of plurality. The Absolute is in no way affected and altered by the phenomenal world. The immutable Reality is ever the same. The Absolute is beyond phenomenal world of nemes and forms. The world changes and passes but the One remains. The acosmic doctrine regards the Absolute as nirguna, attributeless and distinctionless. Its approach is negative and it declares that Brahman never became the universe, and the phenomenal show is only an appearce. It states that sense-perceptions like touch, sound, smell, colour, taste and spatial-temporal qualities, like beginning and end, above and below, right and left, do not apply to the Absolute. The theory of the universe coming out of the Brahman is not a reality. God cannot be charcterized as "this" or "that". An often quoted passage of Madukya Upanishad says, "Not internally conscious, not conscious otherwise, not a mass of consciousness, not conscious, not non-conscious, imperceptible, not amenable to impirical usage, ungraspable, not having an identifying mark, unthinkable, unnamable, the essence of the knowledge of the one Self, that into which all phenomenon get resolved, that which is non-dual-bliss, such they hold, is transcendent Reality."

They hold that the Absolute can be indicated only as "not this, not that". In Brihadaranykopanishad the sage Yajnavalkya says that Brahman cannot be defined by empirical categories. "It is not gross, not subtle, not short, not long, not red, not adhesive, without shadow, without darkness, without air, without space, without attachment, without taste, without smell, without eyes, without ears, without speech, without mind, without light, without breath, without mouth, without measure, and without either inside or outside. It does not eat anything, nor is it eaten by anybody." He is one without second, non-dual, where all empirical usages become meaningless and futile.

In his impersonal, nirguna aspect, Brahman is the eternal witness. He is negation of all attributes. God is the subtlest and most transcendent, He is beyond sense-perception and is not caused by anything except himself. Bereft of attributes he is eternally one and yet becomes many. "For, in him alone, like spokes in a wheel, all the things in the Universe, this earth, the sky, and the intermediary space, the mind, the prana, and the veins, and the arteries are fixed". The concept of non-duality is reached by successive stages and abstractions. The Upanishads were wary not to carry all to the nirguna or attributeless Absolute, irrespective of their mental capacity and spiritual progress. There are various ways for realization for people in various stages of life. They begin with the familiar things. To reach the Supreme Reality one has to pass through many stage and planes. For example, there are personal deities, their cosmic counterparts, than the immanent Brahman with its attributes, and then finally the transcendent Reality, the nirguna or nirupadhika Brahman. Thus, there is no contradiction. Because of nescience the one and the same Reality appears as different and many due to the upadhis or adjuncts. The very idea of plurality is like a dream in which one sees oneself as many. As soon as the dream vanishes, there remains, himself, the only reality in it. The clay deer is not the clay lion, but when dissolved both become clay again. The differences are mere in name and form, not in essence. What is true of Brahman is also true of Individual souls declares the Chandogya Upanishad, "Just as my dear, by one piece of clay everything of clay may be known, the modification is merely a verbal distinction, a name, the reality is just clay".

God, both in his aspects, as saguna and nirguna, is real and essential for the spiritual progress. Both the aspects show that Brahman is the cause and the universe the effect, and that we should concentrate on the cause so that we may be identified with it. That is why Brahman is described both as personal and impersonal, saguna and nirguna, dynamic and static, sopadhika and nirupadhika. But the attributes and Upadhis are mutable, in the sense that they are dependent for their existence on the immutable and nirupadhika Reality. As long as we consider ourselves as embodied beings, we are persons and have

33

personal gods, but when we realize that not only we are Brahman, but the whole creation is Brahman, we transcend all such personal barriers and merge into universal consciousness of transcendence. Then remains only impersonal Reality of the attributeless Absolute.

The Sagunopasna or devotion to the personal God, is a potent means in the ultimate realization of the impersonal Reality. In the ultimate analysis, the Reality is nirguna, changeless and immutable. To reach this highest Reality, one has to pass through lesser indentities of personal deities and grosser, subtler and then to the most subtle. The immence shows the path to transcendence. This synthesis of personal and impersonal aspects of God is expressed in more concrete form in the Bhagvad Gita. Here the immanent and transcendent view-points are beautifully harmonized and reconciled. Here Krishna is presented as personalization of the Upanishadic impersonal Reality, and he is being described in the same language that has been used in the Upanishads to describe the impersonal and immutable Brahman. It is in this context of the cosmic and personal God that devotion, surrender, worship and allegiance become relevant.

God is present in every being, but more so in a person who is awakened, enlightened and godly. That is why it is said that the knower of Brahman is Brahman itself. It is the presence of the virtues that make a man divine, righteous, godly or godlike. One is god himself when godliness is fully manifested through oneself. This marks the only difference between a man and an amoeba, otherwise they stand on the same plane. The avatars of Rama and Krishna are regarded the incarnation of God or ultimate Reality, only because the divinity has found in them the greatest and fullest possible expression. In the Gita Lord Krishna says, "I am the Self, O Gudakesha, seated in the hearts of all beings. I am the beginning, the middle and also the end of all beings. Of the Adityas I am Vishnu; of the luminaries, the radiant Sun; I am Marichi of the Maruts; of the astrisms the Moon am I. Of the Vedas I am Saman; I am Vasava among the Devas; of the senses I am the mind and among the living beings I am consciousness; of beasts I am the lord of beasts, and Vainateya of birds. Of the wielders of weapon I am Rama."

God is in everything, but more so in one person than another in proportion to the manifestation of his glories and divinity. Krishna as incarnation of God is friend to all beings including the Kaurvas, but more so to Arjuna, because through him divinity finds fuller and better expression, because the Pandavas are virtuous and righteous while Kaurvas are not.

The Vedas, the Upanishads and later religious literature of the Hindus are never dogmatic about the relation of the Brahman and the individual Atman. At some places the individual soul is treated as a different entity, but in most of the Hindu religious literature, the identity of both is declared categorically. There may be a difference of opinion on this point, but they are unanimous about the close and abiding relationship between the two, though this relationship is quite subtle and mysterious. They also declare in unison that it is not the body, the senses, the intellect, or the mind which is of supreme importance, but the soul, which is eternal, self-existent, timeless and independent of body. The soul in essence is ever the same and changeless. It is the body which evolves and changes. That is why it is said there is a world of difference between an amoeba and a Buddha on the level of the body, but none whatsoever on the spiritual plane because the same spirit pervades the both, though the degree of the manifestation differs. In Buddha we find the expression of the essence far more greater than in and through an amoeba, like the same water contained in the ocean and a cup.

The Upanishads accept and declare the oneness of Atman, that impersonal Reality and the personal soul and in essence identical. Their diversity is apparent but not real. Their essential oneness is sublimely expressed in the following passage from the Mundakopanishad:

"Two birds, inseparable companions—
In the same tree dwell.
Of the two one eats the sweet fruits,
Uneating the other looks on.
Upon the same tree the soul, overwhelmed,
Grieves at its impotence, bewildered.
When it percieves the Other the infinite Being,
And His splendour, he is freed from grief."

Atman is cosmic breath, not an individual entity, yours and and mine, but universal, beyond senses, intellect and mind, which can be

35

best experiened in deep yogic state of being. The word Atman means soul of the individual and the soul of the universe or cosmos. It is the most subtle, the most transcend and imperceivable by the senses. Atman or soul is self-effulgent and existent, and the senses depend on it for their existence as well as perception. The senses borrow the power of conception only from the soul. Atman is not altered or affected by what appears on it, just as the rope, the shell and the sky appear respectively to be serpent, a silver and a coloured expanse, even so the soul appears to be different on account of the superimposition of the upadhis or adjuncts attributes, not its own.

Atman is fundamntally changeless, one non-dual and all-prevading as the bubbles, the foam and the waves are nothing else but water, of the ornaments are nothing else but the earth though they may be of various forms, sizes and names. The name and the form can never alter the essence of the soul.

The soul is of the nature of consciousness, and all that comes into existence is nothing else but Atman. The individual soul transmigrates in various ways on different planes of existence. The oneness of the soul, the gods and the Supreme Soul is very well expressed in many wellknown hymans and passages, for example, in this hymn of the Rigveda:

"He is the Sun dwelling in the heavens,
the Vayu dwelling in the mid-region,
the priest beside the sacrificial altar.
He is guest in the house, consciousness
in men, the dweller in the noblest
place, dweller in the cosmis order,
born of flood, in the rays of the Sun.
The truth itself."

The existence of universe is based on the identity of the individual soul and the Universal Soul. God is Purusha, and so is man. They both are Purusha in embodied form, and from this manifestation they become impersonal and nirguna Reality. Being most subtle it is described in its negative and positive aspects even in the same hymn. The opposite and self-contradictory terms used in describing Atman shows its indescribleness. In the Chandogya Upanishad Atman is described thus-

"This soul of mine within the heart is smaller than a grain of rice, or a barely corn, or a mustard seed, or a grain of millet.......this soul of mine within the heart is greater then the earth, greater then the atmosphere all the heart is greater than sky, greater than these words." The same thread of Atman runs through and binds together all the beings. The same Atman is manifested through various beings, but prominently so in those beings who are good, godly and beautiful. The immortality of the soul is emphasized in this passage of the Gita—

"The wise grieve not either for

the living or for the dead.

Never was there a time,

when I was not, nor you,

nor any of these princes,

nor is it we shall cease to be in

the future.

The unreal has no existence.

The Real never ceases to be.

The truth about both has

been realized by the seers."

In the Kathopanishad we find Yama, the Lord of Death teaching the young Nachiketas the nature of Atman and the method of its realization. Nachiketas was yet a boy of sixteen; his father Vajsravas performed a sacrifice and gave away in charity to the priests and the Brahmans even such cows which were old, weak, dry and useless. It made Nachiketas sad. He wanted to offer himself in dakshina to undo the wrongful charity of his father and to avoid the possible future misery and punishment to his father. He made up his mind to save his father even at the cost of his own life, and asked Vajsravas thrice to whom he was to go. Twice he did not get any reply, but the third time the father got angry and said, "Go to hell". The boy went to house of Death. Nachiketas remained unattended for three days at the gate of Yama, because the latter was not present there. To atone for this lapse, Yama offered him three boons, and the boy asked Yama as a third favour to be enlightened if after the death of a man there still remained or not the Atman, who is said to be different from the mind, senses and the intellect. Yama tried to dissuade him by offering limitless riches, progeny, kingdom and such other things, but the boy, without being tempted by these attractions, insisted on his boon. And then Yama, finding him a fit and worthy disciple, instructed him in Brahm-vedya or the knowledge of the Self.

"Notwithstanding the bodies being many, there is one universal Atman who is all pervading and immanent in all ....He is at once one and all-pervading....He dwells in the city of the human body. The Atman who can never be emenable to any change, who, being bereft of birth and death, always remains uncontaminated, and as equal to all like the Sun. He does not perish when the body is destroyed. He is beyond the senses and their objects, beyond mind and intellect. Man lives by the presence of Atman on whom depend the senses, the mind and the intellect for their very existence. The Atman alone is the independent element of consciousness and life. Know this Atman ever awake even while the Pranas and senses go to sleep. Know him to be ever pure, imperishable Brahman which is the source and support of all. Just as fire transforms the wood into fire, and assumes itself the shape of the burnt wood even so, the invisible Atman, who is the inner Self of all, becomes manifest and transforms a being into a prototype of himself and assumes for himself the personality and the embodied nature of the devotee, and yet remains as the only transcendent Reality of all."

But the individual sheathed in a body forgets its real nature and identity, and begins to regard itself as a separate soul. Imprisoned in a body, the individual soul feels itself separated and estranged from the Supreme Soul because of nescience. By knowing that there is falling of all fetters, the cessation of the cycle of birth and death. therfore, the highest object of life should be to aim this identification and union with the Brahman. This can be attained only through knowledge and giving up of all works, good as well as evil, for even good actions lead to new births and rebirths. As no water remains attached to the lotus bloom, so no deeds cleave to him who knows Atman. The Bhagvad Gita declares in the same strain—

"He who holds Atman as slayer

and he who regards It as the slain

38

Both of them are ignorant.
It slays not, nor is It slain.
The Atman is neither born,
nor does It die. Coming into being
and ceasing do not take place in It.
Unborn, eternal, constant and ancient
It does not die when the body is slain.
Seek to perform your dharma,
but seek not its fruits.
Be ye not the producer of
The fruits of karma, nor lean towards inaction.
Perform action, O Dhananjaya, being
fixed in yoga, renouncing attachments,
and even-minded in success
and failure: equilibrium is very yoga.
The wise imbued with equanimity
of mind, renouncing the fruits
of their actions, freed from the fetters
of births, verily go to the stainless state."

In the Brihadarankya Upanishad rishi Yajnavalkya, being questioned, tells on many occasions that Atman, like salt in water, is immanent, all-pervading, and all things exist for Atman. Atman is the dearest of all, and all things are dear for the sake of the Atman. The Atman is the most precious, dearer than son, wealth and dearer than all else. therefore, one should meditate on Atman alone for he is only deathless and contemplation on him leads to liberation through dissolution of all desires and actions and the fruits thereof. He who realizes the Atman knowing, "I am He", his pranas do not migrate, they become merged in him, and so there is no return for him. Liberation consists in the realization of the unity of the soul with the Universal Soul.

LIBERATION OR MOKSHA

Moksha or liberation is the highest goal and ideal of Hindu life.

The three other ideals, viz., dharma, artha and karma are secondary, and a means to the summum bonum of the Hindu life, i.e., Moksha or salvation. All the systems and schools of the Hinduism decisively and unanimously declare that moksha, the final liberation, is the loftiest and the ultimate goal of human life. According to one's karma (action) a person is reborn as a particular person. This chain of births and deaths goes on ceaselessly till one obtains moksha by following his dharma dutifully, and through the self-realization. Man is happy or sad according to his past actions. Life is an opportunity for man's spiritual growth and evolution, and the attainment of the ultimate ideal of moksha is the state of identification of the individual soul with the Brahman. It means release from the slavery of the senses and mind. Essentially it is a state of bliss and peace and liberation from the limitations of the phenomenal world. But it never means nothingness or an eternal life of pleasures in heaven.

A jivanmukta, is a person who has already achieved liberation in life iteslf. He is freed from desires; atman is his only desire. Such a man is Brahman and goes to Brahman. He achieves immortality in his very life and realizes the Brahman. there have been many such realized souls in India. Oneness and identity with Brahman is immortality, conquest of death and moksha. Plurality is death. This idea is beautifully expressed in the following four lines from Kathopanishad:

"Wherever he is known, there is truth;

Wherever not known, destruction.

Seeing him in every being,

the sages, departing from here, become immortal."

Moksha is liberation; it is imortality, supreme bliss and eternal peace. Bondage, confinement within limited body, space and time is really death. It is a freedom from limitations, the four walls of physical existence. The Hindu idea of moksha can be seen in the following prayer of Brihadarankya Upanishad:

O thou that are manifest, be Thou manifest to me.

From the unreal lead me to the Real;

From darkness lead me to light,

From death lead me to Immortality.

Thus, moksha is a state of perfection and utmost fulfilment. It is immortality and cessation of birth and death, and the accompanying duality. It cannot be termed as dissolution or destruction of the individual self. It is a state of transcendence and perfection. In the words of Mundaka Upanishad, moksha is "just like the merging of the rivers into the sea, where they lose their name and form. Similarly, the wise, freed from name and form attain the supreme Reality." In Rigveda also we find the same prayer for moksha and immortality. "just as cucumber is removed from its stalk, so from the bondage of Death may I be removed, but not from immortality."

Pointing the path to moksha Kaivalya Upanishad says:-
"He is all, what has been and what shall be,
Having realized him, one overcomes eternal death.
No other path leads to liberation.
When he sees the atman dwelling in all beings
and all beings within the atman, he departs
to the supreme Bahman. there is no other way."

It is the pathway of yoga, which leads an aspirant to final release. Our embodied individual existence is the root of sufferings and death. It is a kind of imprisonment, and the realization of life as one indivisible organic whole, is the only solution of the problem. Before one attains liberation, it is essential that one overcomes the barriers of individual existence, separation and exclusiveness. The final release from the bondage of mundane existence comes only when one realizes the essential unity and divinity of life and atman:

"Only in oneness is to be seen,
the eternal atman, immeasurable
Free from stain is it, beyond space,
unborn, great, unwavering."

The Bhagvad Gita underlines how the performance of actions, without attachment to their fruits, can pave the path to salvation. This is the fundamental message of the Gita. Man cannot live without doing actions, but their fruits ought to be surrendered at the feet of the Lord. It makes a deed devoid of desire or nishkama.

Liberation and release is the enlightened state, it's the attainment of the desired relationship with the Reality. Such an enlightenment requires long and arduous training and practice. It involves a lot of study, reflection, contemplation and realization, preferably under a competent guru. This is the path of yoga. The aim of yoga and accompanying meditation is the realization of the truth by drawing mind from all other things and pinpointing it on the truth. Such a course leads to the direct experience of identity of the soul with the Brahman, and unity of all existence amidst diversity of menifestation. Moksha is a state when all plurality and exclusiveness disappear and all inclusive reality is experienced which is full of absolute peace, bliss and harmony. It is a condition of moral, spiritual and intelectual perfection, and fulfilment, in which all distinctions disappear.

"Where one does not see another, or hear another, or know another, that is fulness. But where one sees another, hears another, knows another, that is limitation. That which is fullness is immortal, but which is limited is mortal,". Such a state is attainable in this very life. This is what the hinduism preaches and urges the aspirants to achieve. Moksha is not hereafter, it is here. Its achievement makes one jivanmukta, a liberated man while still living. There have been many jivanmuktas in ancient and in modern times in India. They meditated on the Self, realised it and became Brahma themselves while still living. King Janaka or Mithila, the father of Sita was one of such jivanmuktas. He became Brahman itself. The great sage Yajanavalakya was his priest and adviser. It is said that they both prepared the way for Buddha. the ignorance or nescience is at the root of bondage. When forgetting our true identity with the Brahman, we begin to identify ourselves with the bodies and its senses and their desires, we are in deep bondage. Our desires, and the actions done to satisfy them, chain the soul. Birth and rebirth are due to desires and the accompanying karma. Hinduism aims at removing the causes which constitute bondage. Moksha is not a post-mortem ideal to be experienced hereafter in the next world. It is to be obtained and experienced here and now. Moksha is the very nature of the soul, and not something to be achieved after death. What prevents the soul from realizing this greatest ideal is avidya or ignorance. As soon as the avidya is dissolved, one becomes videha or jivanmukta.

"When man's desires are dissolved

Which chain his soul, then he

even here becomes immortal, realizing Brahman,"

The Vedic and Upanishadic seers underline the desirability of libration here and now, but it never means that if one fails to obtain enlightenment in this birth can never do so. They firmly believe that every man is bound ultimately to possess this state of supreme bliss and peace. There is no room for despair and hopelessness. The underlying message of hope and cheer, moksha and fulfilment provides enough protection against pessimism. Hinduism is the pathway of inspiring faith, confidence and robust optimism. Those who follow the life of dharma and righteousness, though may not attain final liberaiton in this life, because of some want in respect of efforts and self-control, they are sure to achieve it in stages, and sooner than later. The Hindu sages believe that bliss is the basis of all existence. Ananda is an inherent quality of the Atman, and so there is no need to be depressed by looking at the seamy side of life.

MONOTHEISM AND MONISM

The Vedas and the Upanishads preach and propagate neither pantheism nor polytheism but monotheism and monism. There are many gods like Indra, Varuna, Agni, Mitra, Yama, Brahma, etc., but they represent the different aspects of the same Reality and share some common features and powers. The spirit that pervades these gods is the same. Though One, He is called by many names, such as Indra, or Agni or Mitra. "What is one, the sages call by many names". These gods are lauded and praised in their respective hymns, and it may give the impression that the Vedas advocate pantheism and polytheism, but gradually the idea of one Supreme God crystalizes, and he is seen as the common source of the existence and power of all these gods. For example, Prajapati, the lord of creatures is lauded in some particular hymns as the highest godhead, representing the creative aspect of the supreme Brahman, but later on, when he ceases to represent that aspect of God, he is reduced to the secondary position. Thus, it is clear that reality is one Brahman which is also all-pervading Atman. There are several hymns and passages in the Vedas which may appeaı as polytheistic, but then the omnipresence and omnipotence of the supreme Brahman stressed and underlined explicitly, remove this impression, for example, take this hymn from the Rigveda:

"This was not non-existent nor existent;
there was no realm of air, no sky beyond it.
What covered in, and where? And what gave shelter?
Was water there, Unfathomed depth of water?
Death was not then, nor was there immortal;
no sign was there, aught days and night's divider.
That one Thing, breathless, breathed by
its own nature: apart from it was
nothing whatsoever.
All that existed then was void and formless;
By the great power of Warmth was born the unit."

In these sacred books we find monism and monotheism embracing each other. There are may passages where the ultimate Reality is represented as immanent, while in numerous others as transcendent. The elements of monotheism blend with that of monism so well that sometimes it is difficult to say which is which. But in the Upanishads the trend of monism is more pronounced and conspicuous. The monistic doctrine of the Upanishads admits no other reality except Braham or Atman. Brahma, the all-inclusive first cause of the universe, and that which is the essence of man, are one and the same, they stress that by knowing Brahman all will be known. Brahman as the cosmic principle is the basis of all the individual souls as well as of the whole of the universe. Thus, Upanishads are more monistic and absolutistic than the Vedas. Monism concieves Brahman as the only efficient cause of all existence, while Monotheism represents the personal form of Brahman. But in actuality they are complimentary to each and there is hardly any conflict and contradiction. Brahm in its nirguna and impersonal aspect is one, but as souls and the universe, Braham becomes many. The latter are also real in the sense that they emerge from Brahma. But ultimately Brahmn is the sole reality, the ground and goal of Vedic and Upanishadic teaching. The latter Vedantic definitioin of absolute Reality as Sacchidananda is foreshadowed in the Upanishads. And that famous hymn of Rigveda (X, 129) in which Reality is addressed as "That One" (Tad Ekam), foreshadows the

44

impershonal Brahman of the Upanishads. This One, the only One, is
both personal and impersonal, immanent and transcendent, and they
enrich and make each other more meaningful. In the present context
the following verses may be quoted:

"The sages call him Indra, Mitra, Varuna,

Agni, and he is divine nobly winged Garutman.

To that is One, they give various names,

They call It Agni, Yama, Matarisvan."

(Rigveda I.164.46)

"Its root is above its branches below;
This eternal pipal tree
That indeed is the pure, that is Brahman
that indeed is called the Immortal;
On that do all the worlds rest;
And no one so-ever goes beyond it
This truly is that."

(Katha Upanishad VI.I).

"As a spider might issue forth with its thread,
as small sparks come forth from the fire,
even so from this Soul issue forth
all energies, all worlds and beings."

(Brihada 1.20)

"Not by speech, not by mind
Not by sight can He be apprehended
How can he be apprehended
Otherwise than by one's saying
"He is""

(Kathopanishad VI.12)

"He who thinks himself different
from God, the Lord of all,
goes along with the wheel of Brahman,
which is both the source and dissolution of

all creatures. When the mortal man
with right knowledge can realize
his own identity with Brahman
he enjoy the eternal ananda
even in this very life."

(Svetashvataropanishad 1.6)

"In the beginning this world was
merely non-being. It became
existent; it developed. It turned
into an egg. It lay for a year
before it was split as under."

(Chandogya Upanishad III.19. 1)

"There are assuredly two forms of Brahma: Time and the Timeless.
That which is prior to the sun is Timeless, without parts. But that
which begins with the sun is Time, which has parts."

(Matri Upanishad VI.15)

CHAPTER THREE

The Epics and The Gita

The Ramayana and its sister epic, the Mahabharata constitute a veritable treasure-trove of Indian lore, learning, legends and mythology, both religious and secular. These two great ornate poems, the creation of the heroic age, constitute the national epics of the Hindus. For the last many centuries, these two epics have exercised a profound influence on india's moral and religious living and thinking, and also on all types of creative expression. Puranic in nature, these two great works have been quite popular among the masses. They have percolated through all the strata of Hindu society in the forms of literature, songs, sculpture, painting and classical and folk performing arts. The Vedas and the Upanishads written in Sanskrit were meant for the pandits and scholars, but the epics have been accessible to all and sundry in the form of translations in various vernacular languages of the country. For example, in Hindi alone, which is spoken by the majority of the Indians, there are over 350 versions of the Ramayana. The universal diffusion of the epics in India, nay the whole of the South-east Asia, has been quite wonderful. Their great popularity has been a living monument to the Hindu ideal of ultimate victory of good over evil. They both delineate the eternal principles of dharma and righteous living and triumph over the forces of evil.

In the words of Swami Vivekananda, "The Ramayana and the Mahabharata are the two encyclopaedias of the ancient Aryan life and wisdom, portraying and ideal civilization, which humanity has yet to aspire after". According to Sister Nivedita, "For, it would scarcely be going too far to say that no one unfamiliar with the story of Rama and Sita can be in any real sense a citizen of India, nor acquainted with morality as the greatest of Indian teachers conceived it. Pershps one might go further and say that no one unfamiliar with the story of

47

Rama and Sita can be a true citizen of the world."

Juxtaposing the two epics, Shri P. Lal has very ably observed: "The Ramayana rouses compassion, the Mahabharata almost cosmic awe. The story of Rama and Sita recommends ideal human love, the story of the Pandavas and the Kauravas is a doom narrative. Valmiki rules the Hindus heart, Vyasa goes into his very guts. Valmiki shows the dhammapada, the sweet and straight path of dharma......But Vyasa posits an intricate dharma, where right and wrong are bewilderingly mixed........Valmiki delineates the Hindu, the Indian dream of perfection; Vyasa pricks the Hindu, the Indian conscience. Valmiki's epic is a vision; Vyasa's epic a mirror..... Vyasa is ubiquitious and inescapable, he will not let us be, he is like an eczema itch, a chronic toothache, a betrayed love.

"The anguished intensity of the Indian involvement with the Mahabharata can be seen in the way refererence is made to the epic in public life. the Ramayana is cited generally when ethical ideas are expected, the Mahabharata is referred to when compromises are made, shady deals struck, promises dishonoured, battles fought, disaster lamented."

The Vedas and the Upanishads belonged to the learned. but the epics and the Puranas formed the religious public property. For a long time they were transmitted orally from one generation to another in some particular families of the bards, singers and wandering ministrels. The Ramayana and the Mahabharata can be called the culmination of a long tradition of epic poetry which existed in the Puranic times. By this time many Vedic gods were pushed into background and many others became the part of oblivion, and then Vishnu and Shiva became prominent instead. In the Ramayana and the Mahabharata, it is the heroes Rama and Krishna, the tow incarnations of Vishnu, whose exploits and adventures have been elaborately sung and celebrated. It is the epics and the Puranas which inspire and shape the modern popular hindu thoughts and practice far more than the Vedas and the Upanishads.

The Ramayana is a homogeneous poem and presents much higher idealistic view, and exercises more wide popular appeal than the Mahabharata. Then Ramayana, consisting of seven books and 2,400 shlokas or stanzas, is far shorter in size than the Mahabharata. The Mahabharata, about eight times the size of Iliad and Odyssey put together, the largest of the epics in the world, contains 10,000 verses. The Mahabharata is a whole literature attributed to the pen of rishi Krishna Dwaipayana Vyasa. It is the epics together with the Puranas, which constitute the most mighty single factor that has held together and sustained the Hindus all these centuries full of ups and downs, and foreign racial and political invasions. Their abiding and deep influence on Indian morals, art, culture and the vast gamut of social life is now a well established fact. In the opinion of a scholar the epics "have affected so large a population over so long a period of time and moulded the character and civilization of so vast a region, often transcending geographical limits, can ill afford to be termed mere 'epics'. Indeed the Ramayana and the Mahabharata should better be regarded as true history of India, history not of events, but of urges and aspirations, strivings and purposes of the nation. Encyclopaedic in nature, together they form ' the content of our collective unconscious' wherein breathe 'the united soul of India and the individual soul of her people."

THE RAMAYANA

The Ramayana, composed by rishi and Adi-kavi Valmiki, is an epic of unknown antiquity, but some scholars suppose it to have been created about five centuries B.C. All other Ramayanas and versions including that of Tulsidas (Hindi), and Kamban (Tamil), equally sublime in merit, are based on the original epic of Valmiki. The other well known Ramayana is Krittivasa Ramayana (Bengali). the main message of all these versions have always been the same-the upholding of duty and dharma, and sustenance of order. The Ramayana, a reflection of the highest Hindu ideals, is a sublime textbook of morals and ethics, which has inspired millions and millions of Hindus from time immemorial. It is possessed of many unique facets from which emerge and diffuse the splendid rays of human values and ideals. It has rightly been said that, "As long as the mountains stand and the rivers flow so long shall the Ramayana be cherished among men and save them from sin."

49

The Story of Rama

Once, long long ago, the sage and Adi-kavi Valmiki came to the banks of the river Tamasa for his morning ablutions. There he saw a pair of curlews sporting amorously. Then, there came a fowler and shot the male bird dead with his arrow. Seeing the male bird dead and his mate wailing pitiously, the Rishi's heart was moved with deep compassion and he cursed the fowler. The curse was uttered in even measure and equal feet, and thus the Shloka was born out of Sorrow.

Valmiki returned to his ashrama, but the shloka continued to revolve in his mind. Just then Brahma, the four-faced Creator appeared in person, and told Valmiki to relate the entire story, the heroic exploits of Rama in verse, for he himself had inspired that poetic utterance. Brahma blessed the sage with the vision that had happened in public or privately in Rama's life, and told him that nothing he related would be untrue, and that as long as the rivers and the mountains were there on the earth, so long would the Rama-story last in the world. Brahma disappeared leaving Valmiki full of awe and wonder. He sang and repeated the Shloka, and then began to compose the Ramayana. He set into deep meditation and envisioned all that had happened in the life of Lord Rama. He saw everything with the eye of his mind as one would behold a fruit held on one's plam.

The Ramayana is Composed

He composed the entire Rama katha in the verse form so ravishing to the ear and mind, and so full of noble deeds and thoughts as the ocean is full of rare gems. Having composed the Ramayana in the epic form of twenty four thousand verses, he fell wondering as how and by whom it could be propagated throughout the world. As he was musing thus, there came Lava and Kusha, the two young princes, possessed of sweet melodious voice, and well versed in all the sacred lore. He taught them the great epic and bade them to recite the same to the accompaniment of Veena. They sang the story before the learned audience and the assembly of receptive people. They would hear with rapt attention, with their hearts full of joy and the eyes pearld with tears. Once Rama chanced to see these honey-tongued princes recite the sacred lay, and invited them to sing it in his august court. There they recited the entire epic before the whole royal audience.

Dasharatha's Ayodhya

The famed and fair Ayodhya, the capital city of the kingdom of Koshala, stood on the banks of the sacred Saryu river. It was unconquerable by war or weapon. There ruled Dasharatha, the illustrious king of the solar race. Ayodhya rivalled Indra's Amravati in opulence and beauty. The king ruled over his righteous subjects with the help of his wise ministers and counsellors. But the king felt sad on the score that he had no son to continue the line and inherit the kingdom. It gnawed into his vitals. One day he decided to perform the Horse Sacrifice to obtain a son with the wise assistance and guidance of the priests and the counsellors. He invited Rishyashringa, the best of the rishis, to preside over the sacrifice. The next year in the spring season, the Ashvamedha sacrifice began under the guidance of Rishyashringa and Vashishtha. Consequently, Dasharatha received the boon of four sons, and it exceedingly delighted his heart and those of his three Queens.

The Princes are Born

Six season and eleven months had gone by, and then in the twelfth month of Chaitra, in the very auspicious zodiacal signs, the eldest queen Kaushalya gave birth to Rama, the lotus-eyed and long-armed prince. And queen Kaikeyi gave birth to righteous Bharata, and the youngest queen Sumitra to twin sons Lakshmana and Shatrughna, possessed of one-quarter of Lord Vishnu's essence. There were great rejoicings and festivities at their birth. Soon the four princes grew into heroes and valiant fighters and mastered the Vedas and other scriptures. The king immensely rejoiced in these and thought of their marriage, as they stood on the threshold of manhood.

One day, Vishvamitra, a great rishi came to Dasharatha and asked a favour of sending with him Rama and Lakshmana to protect his sacrifice from the demons. The two demons Maricha and Subahu spoiled and polluted his sacrifice urged by Ravana. Dasharatha was not ready to send the two princes with the sage for such a dangerous enterprise. The King instead offered his services and those of his army, but Vishvamitra insisted on taking away Rama, for only he could destroy the demons. Vishvamitra assured the king of Rama's certain victory and their safe return. Vashistha advised Dasharatha to send Rama with Vishvamitra, as no harm could come to the prince under the sage's protection, and moreover Rama himself was more than a match to these devils.

The Initiation of Marriage

Vashistha blessed, and Dasharatha smelt the head of Rama and Lakshmana and committed them to the sage's care. Armed with bows and arrows, they followed the sage. When they reached the southern bank of the river saryu, Vashistha taught the princes some spells to overcome hunger, fatigue, disease and old age. Having mastered the mantras, Rama shone like the autumnal sun. Soon they reached a dark, deep and fearful forest, and there Rama slew the sinful demoness Tadaka at Vishvamitra's behest. Soon they arrived at Siddha Ashrama, the hermitage of Vishvamitra. The next day, the sacrifice began while the princes kept the vigil. The sacrifice progressed smoothly for five days, but on the sixth day at once a terrible noise arose accompanied by deep darkness, and Maricha and Subahu came sweeping down to spoil the sacrifice. They rained blood, marrow and bones on the altar, but soon Rama slew Subahu and hurled Maricha headlong into the sea, a hundred yojanas away without killing him. having achieved their object of overcoming the demons and the successful completion of the sacrifice, the princes went to Mithila, the capital of Raja Janaka, led by their guru Vishvamitra. There the guru wanted to show his two royal disciples the famed and wonderful bow of Lord Shiva, which none had been able to raise and string.

They set out for Mithila to witness the wonderful and mighty bow, and janaka's great sacrifice. During the journey, Vishvamitra told the princes many interesting ancient stories and legends. When they reached the outskirts of the city, they beheld a beautiful but deserted ashrama of rishi Gautama. There Rama redeemed Gautama's wife Ahalya of the curse under which she had been lying unseen and

invisible to the eye of men and the gods.

Janaka received Vishvamitra with great honour due to him. Vishvamitra introduced the two princes, and requested the king to show them the mighty bow of Shiva, which janaka did with a very glad heart. The bow was brought on the eight-wheeled cart dragged by five thousand powerful men. Relating how he came to possess that wonderful bow, Janaka told them how the gods, gandharvas, demons and mighty kings and princes had failed to string it, and how he had resolved to bestow his beloved daughter Sita only on him who bowed and bent the bow. With the permission of Janaka and the blessings of his guru, Rama took out the bow from its chest, and tried to draw and string it. Rama bent and strung it effortlessly in full view of all the spectators till at last it broke into two, snapping from the middle. It mightily gladdened the hearts of all the people of Mithila, and fast messengers were sent to Ayodhya with the happy tidings of Rama's marriage. King Dasharatha arrived accompanied by his mighty army, ministers, priests and others. Sita's hand was placed in that of Rama in marriage. Bharata, Lakshmana and Shatrughna were also married then and there to the princesses Mandvi, Urmila and Shrutakirati respectively.

Dasharatha's Desire

Dasharatha loved his four sons more than his own life, but Rama was the dearest, for his excellent qualities of head and heart. He decided to install Rama as the heir-apparent and crown-prince. He wanted to see the virtuous Rama as the King before he died. In consultation with the guru Vashistha, ministers, priests, other wise people and the public, Rama's installation as the Regent Prince was decided, and the grand preparations were ordered. The decision sent a rapturous wave through the hearts of the entire kingdom, but the maid Manthara was an exception. She was the favourite maid-attendant of the queen Kaikeyi. When the hunch-backed maid came to know about Rama's installation on the throne, she rushed to Kaikeyi burning with jealousy, and poisoned her ears by her malicious advice. At first Kaikeyi resisted her ill-advice, but ultimately gave, in and her jealousy was roused. Then Manthara reminded Kaikeyi of the two boons the

King had granted her long ago, and she has reserved them for future. Manthra advised Kaikeyi to ask for the immediate installation of her son Bharata on the throne, and banishment of Rama into the forest for fourteen years.

Kaikeyi in the Wrath-Chamber

Thus advised and beguiled, Kaikeyi rose from her uxurious couch with her burning sighs and resolved to adopt that course of ruin. She, the most loved one, of the wild eyes, went straight to the Chamber of Displeasure and lay there on the bare floor, having thrown away all her jewels and ornaments. In the meantime, Dasharatha came himself to the Kaikeyi's palace to convey the happy news, but finding her not there, and learning that she has been taken herself to the Chamber of Wrath, he rushed thither extremely agitated. Dasharatha addressed her in most loving words and caressed her foundly, but she, bent upon evil, did not respond at all.

When Dasharatha had sworn by Rama and said that he would grant whatever she desired, she felt reassured and said, "Install Bharata on the throne, and send Rama into exile in the Dandaka forest as an ascetic" Stunned by her cruel words, Dasharatha fell into a swoon. When he recovered he prayed Kaikeyi with folded hands not to exile Rama, his very life, but she remained relentless and inexorable. Lamenting bitterly, Dasharatha pleaded in vain with her for mercy. While he writhed in anguish, she kept on taunting him in the name of dharma and righteousness. Sumantra came to inform Dasharatha that everything was ready for Rama's coronation, but the king could not say anything out of profound sorrow. Kaikeyi then sent Sumantra to bring Rama there. Rama immediately drove to Kaikeyi's palace, and was dismayed to find his father sunk in deep gloom and dejection. Rama asked Kaikeyi why the king was in dejection. She shamelessly told Rama about her two boons and asked him to redeem the king's pledges by going into exile for fourteen years leaving the throne for Bharata.

Rama is Exiled

It deeply grieved Rama that Keikeyi thought he would not obey his father. Rama instantly agreed to go to the forest for fourteen years as a hermit to redeem his father's pledges. Rama went round his unconscious father and Kaikeyi in reverence and hastened to his palace to take leave of his mother. When people came to know about Rama's banishment, they wept and lamented aloud and sank into sorrow. The terrible news struck mother Kaushalya like lightning, and she fell into a swoon. Rama raised her gently, and when she came to her senses Rama prevailed upon her to allow him to go in exile in obedience to his father's command.

Sita insisted to accompany Rama to the forest and said, "O Raghava, if you do not take me with you, I shall take recourse to poison, fire or water to terminate my life". So, Rama agreed to take her with him. Lakshmana also begged Rama with tearful eyes to take him into the exile, and Rama had to agree. They gave away all their wealth, chariots, steeds and other possessions in charity and went to king Dasharatha to bid him final farewell. Dasharatha blessed and reluctantly allowed Rama to repair to the forest. Clad in ascetic's garb, Rama, Lakshmana along with Sita departed for the forest. The celestial weapons they carried dazzled the eyes of the beholders. It was a very painful parting and the earth got drenched with tears. A great number of citizens, including old and venerable Brahmans followed Rama's chariot on foot. So, Rama got down from his chariot and walked on foot. They reached the river Tamasa and spent the night there.

Rama got up early before dawn and finding the people fast asleep, being tired, left the place immediately to spare the people the hardships of the journey. Rama travelled fast and reached the last limits of Koshala. Soon they reached the banks of the sacred river Ganga and decided to spend the night there. There came Guha, the Nishad King to welcome Rama. The next morning Rama bade Guha farewell and crossed Ganga in a boat. Before that Rama had sent back Sumantra, the charioteer, to Ayodhya. Travelling leisurely on foot they arrived at Bhardwaja's hermitage and were received with great hospitality. The next morning Rama took leave of the sage and set out for Chitrakuta. Having reached Chitrakuta, Lakshmana built a beautiful hut and they dwelt there for some time.

Dasharatha's Death

Treavelling fast, Sumantra, the charioteer returned to Ayodhya with a heavy heart, and found the city ominous, sickly and cheerless. He found the people in groups mourning Rama's departure. Sumantra speedily went to Dasharatha's place and conveyed to him Rama's salutation and the message. The king overwhelmed with grief fell into a swoon and lay motionless on the ground. When he recovered, he wept and cried for his exiled son and died soon after at midnight. Ayodhya was plunged in deep sorrow and great confusion. The corpse of the king was embalmed and it was decided that Bharata should be installed king. Swift messengers, on horses were despatched to bring Bharata and Shatrughna from Kekaya, the capital of Bharata's maternal grand father. That night Bharata had a dreadful dream, and so was very much disturbed in spite of himself.

Worried and responding to urgent call from Ayodhya, Bharata rode with speed. On the way he met many ominous signs and was filled with misgivings. On learning about virtuous Rama's exile and his father's death because of Rama's separation, from his own mother's mouth, he fell down on the earth struck down by grief crying, "Alas, I am undone!" Plunged in 'fathomless grief, he refused to be crowned and reproached his mother crying piteously. Having performed the funeral rites of his father Dasharatha with all solemnity, Bharata set out for the forest to request Rama to return and to ascend the throne.

Bharata Meets Rama

The army was ordered to march. Bharata drove fast eager to see Rama. The queens, ministers, priests and the citizens in great number accompanied him. They arrived at Sringberpura and were accorded a warm welcome by the Nishad king, Guha. The next day they arrived at saint Bhardwaja's ashrama and spent the night there, and then set out for Chitrakuta. Bharata went ahead of all and fell down at Rama's lotus feet, with his voice choked with tears. Rama raised Bharata up and embraced him and enquired about Dasharatha's well being. Bharata told him how their father had expired overcome with grief of Rama's separation, and prayed Rama to return to Ayodhya to occupy the throne, but Rama remained steadfast and inexorable in his vow to remain into exile. Then, Bharata requested Rama for his sandals. Rama took off the sandals and gave them to the noble and high souled Bharata. Bharata bowed before them and then placing them on his head returned to Ayodhya. Bharata placed the sandals under the royal umbrella and administered justice and royal business in Rama's name and lead an ascetic's life.

In the meantime Rama left chitrakuta and visited the sage Atri and his wife Anusuya. Having taken leave of the great ascetic, Rama entered the dense Dandaka Forest as does the sun a great mass of dark clouds. They pressed on, Rama leading, Lakshmana following and Sita walking between them. They met rishis, ascetics and anchorites and spent as many as ten years among them. The ascetics complained against the demons and sought his protection against these night-rangers. Rama along with Sita and Lakshmana visited the hermitages of rishis Sarabhanga and Suitkshna, and finally they came to the great sage Agastya's ashrama. The holiest of the sages, Agastya was greatly delighted to receive Rama and gave him a divine sword and a never failing bow of Vishnu and many celestial arrows.

Sita is Abducted

Finally, Rama came to Panchavati, a fascinating spot on the bank of the river Godavari. There Lakshmana raised a pleasant hermitage of ample size with beams of bamboo and thatched it with grass and leaves. There they dwelt happily, and then there came one day Surpanakha, Ravana's sister. She requested Rama to be her lord and husband. Refused by Rama, she turned to Lakshmana and prayed him to make her his wife. This enraged Lakshmana, and he cut off her nose and ears. Bleeding and howling, she fled to Khara, Ravana's younger brother, who ruled in nearby Janasthana. Khara sent his huge army to destroy Rama, Lakshmana and Sita, but Rama soon slew the entire army with its generals. Then Khara himself set out leading an army of fourteen thousand great warriors. A terrible battle ensued, but then Rama destroyed them all with his deadly arrows.

Now, Surpanakha approached Ravana wailing and weeping, and showed him her wounds. Taunting him, she urged Ravana to avenge the death of Khara by abducting Sita. She advised him to make beautiful and blameless Sita his wife. Determined to carry off Sita, he went to see Maricha, and asked his help in the abduction of Sita. Maricha tried his best to dissuade Ravana from that evil design, but Ravana remained adamant and threatened Maricha with death in case he refused to help him. Out of fear, Maricha became the bejewelled golden dear and began to frisk about at the entrance of Rama's cottage. Sita was fascinated by it and requested Rama either to catch or kill the deer for her. Rama ran after the deer with the bow in his hand. The magic deer led Rama far away. At last Rama let a deadly arrow fly from his mighty bow. It sped like lightning and slew the deer. While dying, Maricha transformed himself into his real self and cried aloud in Rama's voice "Alas Sita! Alas Lakshmana!"

Sita heard the distress call and urged Lakshmana to go to Rama's help. She forced Lakshmana to go with many bitter reproaches. Lakshmana knew that Rama was invincible and not in any danger at all, but he was helpless and so, he had to go. When Ravana saw Sita alone and helpless, he came before her in the guise of a mendicant. Sita taking him to be a sage offered water and fruits. Ravana bent upon sin and evil abducted Sita and carried her off forcibly. When Jatayu, the king of the birds saw Ravana thus abducting Sita, he challenged Ravana and fought a fierce battle, but being old Jatayu got at last worsted and Ravana cut off his wings, flanks and feet with his sharp sword. He lay there fatally wounded, and Ravana carried off wailing and weeping Sita. Ravana drove fast in his aerial chariot absorbed in his thoughts. Sita dropped her jewels on the peak of a mountain as a token unnoticed by Ravana, when she saw some monkeys there. Ravana kept faultless Sita in the Ashoka Grove in Lanka.

Rama and Lakshmana returned to the ashrama, but found it without Sita. Rama was plunged in sorrow and remained unconsolable. They searched Sita in every place but all in vain. Suddenly they found Jatayu, who lay dying in a pool of blood. Jatayu told Rama how Ravana had stolen Sita, and how he tried to rescue Sita and was fatally wounded in the fight. Rama embraced the dying royal bird and then cremated him. Searching Sita, they arrived at Shabari's ashrama. She received them with due courtesies and offered them water and forest fruits. Resuming their journey they arrived on charming Pamapa's banks.

Friendship with Sugriva

Soon they reached the Rishyamooka mountain, where dwelt Sugriva with Hanuman and his other ministers. Sugriva was living there in exile, driven out of Kishkindha by his elder brother vali. Hanuman escorted Rama to Sugriva's presence and they befriended each other. Sugriva told how he was deprived of his dear wife by Vali and was living in exile. He prayed Rama to relieve him from that dread and to restore his wife. In return he promised to recover Sita. Sugriva showed Rama the jewels of Sita which she had dropped there while being carried by Ravana. Rama slew Vali and installed Sugriva on the throne of Kishkindha. The rainy season being over, Sugriva sent monkey hosts in all the directions under mighty leaders for the search. But Sugriva relied more on Hanuman, and gave him some special instructions. Rama also felt that Hanuman would be successful in the enterprise, and so gave him his signet ring as a token.

Hanuman along with Angada and others pressed forward, exploring all the places and arrived at the seashore. There they came to know from Sampati, Jatayu's younger brother that he had seen Sita being carried off to Lanka by Ravana. Lanka was a hundred yojanas across the sea. The monkeys held a debate to ascertain as who of them could leap over to Lanka and come back safely. Each of the great monkeys declared one by one how far he could leap and dare. Thus, the debate went on and finally it was decided that Hanuman was the best choice for the venture. Hanuman got ready and grew into an immense and formidable size. Having resolved, Hanuman leapt into the sky and landed on the other side of the sea.

Hanuman in Lanka

Hanuman, the foremost of the apes, entered Lanka at night assuming a tiny form. It was a splendid city perched on Trikuta hill, girt with golden walls and wide moats. Hanuman searched every mansion and palace for Sita, but saw her nowhere. He then entered Ravana's royal palace full of lovely princesses and splendour, which looked like the paradise. There he saw Ravana sprawling on a golden bed in sound sleep and beside him on a separate bed, a lovely moon-complexioned lady. She was Mandodari, Ravana's chief queen.

Hanuman continued his search and at last reached the Ashoka Grove. There he saw Sita under Ashoka tree, in single soiled cloth. She looked like a tongue of flame obscured by smoke, guarded by fierce Rakshasis.

Hidden behind the thick foliage, Hanuman saw Ravana coming followed by many lovely ladies. He approached Sita and wooed her in many ways, but Sita trembling all this while like a plaintain leaf, refused to respond to his love and warned that he was sure to die at Rama's hands soon. It enraged Ravana beyond measure, and he threatened Sita with death if she did not agree to be his wife within two months. When Ravana had departed and Sita was left alone, Hanuman approached her most humbly and told her that he was sent by Rama, and gave her Rama's signet ring. She was greatly relieved and pleased that Rama and Lakshmana were well, and blessed Hanuman profusely. Sita gave Hanuman her message for Rama and also her crest jewel as a token. Hanuman wanted to be allowed to carry Sita on his back to Rama, but Sita did not think it proper, as it would do no credit to Rama that she should be rescued by Hanuman. So, Hanuman took leave of Sita, but then he decided to ascertain the powers of the foe. With this object in mind he destroyed the pleasure garden of Ashoka and killed its guards. Ravana sent many warriors to capture Hanuman, but Hanuman slew them all. Finally came Indrajit, the son and a warrior of great renown. After great efforts on the part of Indrajit, Hanuman deliberately allowed himself to be captured. He was brought before Ravana in his court. There Hanuman saw Ravana in his full royal splendour and pomp. Hanuman told Ravana to follow dharma and to return Sita, but Ravana beside himself with rage ordered that Hanuman's tail should be set ablaze as punishment.

The Rakshasas soaked Hanuman's tale in oil and fat and set it on fire. Hanuman swelled into a formidable size and scaled the lofty mansions and palaces with his burning tail, and thus spread the conflagration. The big fire spread everywhere aided by the swift wind. Having burnt down the city of Lanka, Hanuman quenched the fire on his tail in the sea, and then in a mighty leap returned to his friends on the other side of the sea. All the apes and bears and their chiefs collected around Hanuman, and heard him with great joy relate his adventures in Lanka. In a very happy frame of mind they returned to Rama on Prasravana hill, and bowed their heads at his feet. Hanuman gave Rama. Sita's message and her crest jewel and related all that happened there in Lanka during his sojourn. Rama held Sita's jewel against his heart, and weeping in joy embraced Hanuman again and again.

The Great March

The high-souled Raghava praised Hanuman for his wonderful achievement, but felt sad to think how the monkey army would cross over the sea. Sugriva comforted Rama with inspiring words, and then the mighty hosts of apes were ordered to march. They reached the shore of the sea, and its din drowned the roar of the sea. Rama summoned a council and discussions were held as how to cross the sea. In the meanwhile, Vibhishana, Ravana's younger and saintly brother, came to Rama seeking refuge and joined him. Ravana had insulted Vibhishana when he advised Ravana wisely to send Sita back. It was decided that Rama should seek the Ocean's help for constructing a causeway. Rama prayed for three days, but there was no response from the Ocean. Rama got furious and was about to dry up the sea when the Sea-god appeared from the ocean-depths with joined palms and begged Rama's forgiveness. He told Rama that there was Nala, Vishvakarma's son, a skilled ape in his army, who could construct a causeway across the sea, which the Ocean promised to bear up.

Nala was immediately summoned and ordered to construct the bridge. The apes sprang on their feet and ransacked the forest for timber. They pulled and broke off the mountain peaks and within six days Nala completed the wonderful bridge over that hundred yojana stretch of the sea. The monkey army crossed over the sea along the bridge and camped on the southern shore. When Ravana heard of the causeway and the crossing over of the sea, he was wonder-struck. He found Lanka besieged by the monkeys. Beside himself with rage, he ordered his army to march and a terrible battle ensued.

The Great Battle

The apes and the Rakshasas clashed and the battle grew fiercer. They fought many terrible duels and single combats. The sun went down but the fight continued. Indrajit, Ravana's great warrior son, using magic tactics wounded Rama and Lakshmana at many places remaining himself invisible. He finally immobilized both the heroes with a shower of his sharp arrows, and returned in triumph to Lanka. Vibhishana rallied the monkey forces and said encouraging words to Sugriva. In the meantime Rama recovered, but finding Lakshmana seemingly dead, lamented piteously. But then there appeared Garuda, the king of the birds. As Garuda came near, the sharp snake-arrows fell from the wounded Rama and Lakshmana. He touched their bodies, and they were healed of their wounds and regained their former vigour and strength, and even more.

When Ravana heard of the princes's recovery and their release from the Nagapasha, he could not believe his ears. He sent Durmukha, a valiant Rakshasha as the head of a great army. He fought fiercely but then finally Hanuman slew him with a huge rock. Ravana then sent many other great Rakshasa warriors, but Ravana was humbled and humiliated again and again by Rama and his army. Ravana then sent his brother Kumbhakarna to give the fight. he looked like the god of Death itself, and the earth shook under his tread. He was huge like a mountain. He caused havoc in the ape army and killed thousands of them. The rocks broke against his mountainous body and the trees were smashed. He wounded Hanuman and struck Sugriva unconscious and carried him away to lanka. But then Sugriva recovered and cutting off his ears and nose with his teeth and nails got away, and the battle began afresh. Kumbhkarna rushed at Rama, but Rama with his sharp arrows deprived him of his weapons and then cut off both his arms. Then Rama shot a splendid Indra arrow with the speed of thought. It lit up the whole atmosphere and went hissing and cut off Kumbhakarna's mountainous head. His trunk reeled and toppled down crushing thousands of apes. The routed Rakshasa army fled to Lanka in panic and told Ravana about his brother's death.

Sunk in deep sorrow, he bewailed his mighty brother's death and fainted. When he recovered from the swoon and sat brooding over the death of his so valiant sons, brothers, chiefs and others at Rama's hands, there came his son Indrajit. He said, "Stop grieving, O father and king, for still I am alive. None can escape my deadly shafts." Indrajit rode again to the war and massacred the apes in the fight. He made himself invisible and wrought havoc among the enemy forces. His arrows were seen but not their author himself. Under his onslaught of arrows even Rama and Lakshmana fell down senseless and dead to all appearances. The monkey chiefs were totally confused and stupified. Then Hanuman sped to the Himalaya mountain and brought from there the life-saving wonder-herbs. The princes inhaled the wonder-herbs and soon were completely healed. They woke up as if from a sleep.

The battle began again the next day, and Indrajit again restored to his maya-tactics, he had a phantom Sita with him, whom he slew in the full view of the monkeys. Hearing of Sita's death Rama fell in a swoon, deluged in grief. Vibhishana came there and saw Rama lying unconscious. Vibhishana then told Lakshmana, Hanuman and Sugriva about Indrajit's magic and the phantom Sita. He assured them that Sita was very much alive and safe for Ravana would never allow her to be slain. Encouraged with these words of hope, Lakshmana went straight where Indrajit was performing a sacrifice and challenged him to a battle. Lakshmana engaged Indrajit in a terrible battle and then finally despatched him to the abode of Death with his deadly missiles. The Rakshasas fled pell-mell and reported to Ravana his son's tragic end.

Ravana Slain

It was too much for Ravana, and he fainted. Coming to his senses, he wailed loud and long inconsolably. His sorrow changed into wrath and then mounting a splendid car he rode to the battle, accompanied by many mighty giants. As he moved, the earth quaked, the sun grew pale and the sky was enveloped in darkness. Ravana of the formidable strength, wrought havoc, and even monkey-chiefs fled in terror before him. Rama stretched his bow taut and rent his dreaded arrows. The gods from above saw Rama on foot and Ravana on his car. They felt the fight was unequal, and so Indra, the lord of the gods, immediately sent his celestial car for Rama. Rama bowed before and then mounted the car. A wonderous duel ensued between the two heroes like between the two lions. Both the armies stood motionless and marvelling with their hair standing on end, and witnessed the final encounter spellbound. It fascinated the gods and they exclaimed. "The sky is like the sky, and like none else. The sea can be compared only to sea. So is the duel peerless between Rama and Ravana, like the heroes themselves". Rama took a razor sharp snke-arrow and with it cut off one of Ravana's ten heads, but instantly another sprang up in its place. Rama severed hundred heads of Ravana, and hundred other sprang up of his shouldrs. It filled Rama with wonder and the fight went on for seven days and nights ceaselessly. Finally, Rama shot the most dreaded missile presided over by Brahma, given to him by the great sage Agastya. The wind was in its feathers, the sun and the moon in its might, and its body was that of space (akasha). Its weight was equal to mountains. The lethal arrow went hissing with the speed of thought and piercing Ravana's chest, cleft his heart, and he fell dead on the ground. Ravana's funeral rites were performed by his brother Vibhishana with due honours.

The Fire Ordeal

Vibhishana conducted Sita in a planqin reverently before Rama's presence. He and his attendants drove away the crowd of monkeys, bears and Rakshasas, but Rama stopped it and ordered Sita to be brought on foot in the full view of the crowd. Sita came and stood before Rama, but rama spoke to her harshly saying that he had redeemed the honour of his family by defeating the foe, and that he took all the trouble not for her sake, but to wipe away the insult done to his fair name. He said, that he could not take her back as she had lived long in another's house. These cruel words of Rama stunned the great assembly, and Sita shed a flood of tears, trembling in shame. Sita then said, "O hero, why do you speak like a common man? I did not come into another's contact out of my desire, I was helpless. My heart was mine and it is still pure and chaste. You have utterly failed to understand my exalted birth and nature, I am earth-born Sita."

She immediately got a pyre prepared and entered into it, as she did not want to live in shame and false accusation. The great assembly was horrified. Then the gods appeared and proclaimed in one voice Sita's innocence and purity. Rama was immensely happy at this and weeping in joy said, "I knew Sita is chaste and pure, but fire ordeal was essential to convince the people of her sinlessness". Agni, the fire-god rose from the blazing fire with resplendent Sita in his lap, and offered her back to Rama. Rama got up and embraced Sita. Rama then returned to Ayodhya with the blessings of the gods in the Pushpaka Viman. He was accompanied by Vanara chiefs. Bharata met Rama and offered him his worship and washed his feet. Then, Bharata restored the kingdom to Rama most humbly.

The Coronation of Rama

Rama's matted locks were trimmed by expert hair dressers. Lakshmana, Bharata and Shatrughna also got rid of their tangled and matted locks. Rama was escorted to Ayodhya in a splendid car and a grand procession from Nandigram, and installed on the throne with the chanting of Vedic hymns by guru Vashistha, helped by other sages. Sita sat on the throne beside Rama shining in her effulgence. Rama gave away suitable presents of Jewels, gold, silver, money, steeds, elephants, milch-kine, bulls and rich robes to Vanara chiefs, Brahmaans, priests, Vibhishana and to others. Rama made Bharta Yuvaraja and his junior, and ruled justly like his great ancestors for a long time performing holy rites and many sacrifices, including the great Horse-sacrifice. The people lived happily leading a virtuous life full of dharma.

THE STORY OF THE PANDAVAS

Chitrangada, the elder son of Shantanu and Satyavati died in the battle with the Gandharva King. Then, the young Vichitravirya was made King, and Bhishma acted as regent. When Vichitravirya came of age he was married to Ambika and Ambalika, the two priencesses of Kashi, but before long he died childless and there was none to continue the line and inherit the kingdom. In desperation Satyavati requested Bhishma to marry one of the widowed queens, but he of the "terrible vow" refused to oblige. Then, Satyavati remembered her pre-marriage island-born son Vyasa from rishi Prahara.

Rishi Vyasa agreed to oblige his mother by entering into the two widowed queens. He first went to Ambika, but she was so terrified with his repulsive visage that she closed her eyes tight, and consequently gave birth to blind Dhritarashtra. When Vyasa went to Ambalika, she was scared and grew pale in the process. And gave birth to pale complexioned Pandu. Since Dhritarashtra was blind, Bhishma made pandu the King. In due course of time Dhritarashtra was married to Gandhari, and Pandu to Kunti and Madri. Kunti gave birth to Yudhishthira, Bhima and Arjuna. From Madri were born Nakula and Sahdeva. To Dhritarashtra and Gandhari were born a hundred sons and a daughter, and Duryodhana was the eldest son. When Pandu died, Madri became sati by ascending his funeral pyre. The Kaurava and Pandu princes began to grow up together, but soon the Kaurava princes began to harbour a childish illwill for their cousins.

The Coming of Dronacharya

Kripacharya was the first tutor of the princes. When they became proficient in archery and other arts, some more skilled teacher was needed, and Dronacharya was appointed their teacher. He taught the princes the all kinds of weapons, human and divine, along with his son Asvathama. Drona had determined to make Arjuna the best archer because of his deep devotion to him. One day he put his pupils to a test by placing a clay bird high up a tree, and asked them to come forward one by one with their bows and arrows. Yudhisthira was the first to come but he failed to answer the question satisfactorily asked by Drona, and so he was asked to step aside. The other princes also fared poorly to answer the question. Arjuna was the last to come. He answered the questions correctly, and so Drona said to Arjuna, "Shoot at the bird", and instantly came down the bird struck by Arjuna's arrow.

The Tournament

When the princes had completed their education and training, a royal tournament was held to publicly exhibit the princes, skills and powers. The princes performed wonderful feats; Bhima and Duryodhana gave an excellent performance in the duel of maces, but when this mock fight began to verge on a real one, it was instantly stopped. Arjuna, the best of the archers, gave an excellent performance with bow and arrow. The crowd applauded Arjuna again and again.

But Karna performed the same feats with equal perfecetion and challenged Arjuna to a single combat. Both of them stood ready for the duel, but then it was not allowed, because Karna's royal lineage was not known seemingly. Karna was the son of a charioteer Adhiratha.

Duryodhana immediately came forward, and made Karna the king of Anga. And thus a permanent bond of friendship was forged between the two. When Bhima said sarcastically to Karna, "You, a charioteer's son, are not fit even to be killed by Arjuna". Duryodhana felt angry and took away Karna by the hand, and making him sit in the chariot drove away.

In fact, Karna was Kunti's own son, and thus the Pandava's elder brother, but nobody knew this secret. Kunti had a boon. By it she could summon any god to make love with her and obtain a son. When she was a mere girl, and out of curiosity she invoked the Sun-god. She begged Surya's forgiveness, but the boon would not be ineffectual, and so out of this union, a son was born to her wearing a divine armour of gold and resplendent ear-rings. Being unmarried, Kunti was much afraid. She wrapped the baby-son in silk, placed in a wooden box and set it adrift in the yamuna. The chest containing the child was washed ashore, and then it was picked up by childless couple, Adhiratha and his wife Radha. They named him Karna and brought up as their own son.

The Lac-Lalace

Yudhisthira being the eldest, was made heir-apparent to the throne. This coupled with the Pandava's popularity and excellence, made the Kauravas all the more jealous. They always invented ways and means to humiliate and destroy their mighty cousins. Dhritarashtra, the doting father failed to discipline his sons, rather connived at their scheming. They prepared a mansion of lac and other highly inflammable materials, and invited the Pandavas to live there during a celebration. The Pandavas started for the mansion, but the wise Vidura, their uncle forewarned the Pandavas of the lurking danger in a language intelligible only to Yudhisthira. But the Pandavas did not want to precipitate the matter by showing that they knew the plot, however, they were on their guard.

At dead of night the Pandavas with their mother Kunti escaped through a secret tunnel dug out especially for this purpose during their stay in the house. While escaping, Bhima had set the mansion on fire with a flaming torch. It was believed that the Pandavas had died in the fire alive.

The Pandavas Win a Bride

The Pandavas reached Ekachakra and there lived disguised as Brahmans. When they heard about Panchala princess Draupadi's Syayamvara, they set out for Kampilya, the capital of Drupada. When they reached the place of Svayamvara, Duryodhana with Karna was already there. The splendid hall was packed to capacity with princes, who had come to try their luck. Then princess Draupadi was led into the hall. Bejewelled, she looked like a goddess. Then Draupadi's brother Dhristadyumna declared. "Here is bow and five arrows, and above there the target. One who hits the target with these five arrows wins my sister's hand in marriage". Then he told her sister the lineage of the royal princes assembled there. The princes came one by one. And tried their utmost, but utterly failed. Then came Karna, he bent and strung the bow, took aim and was about to shoot the target, the Pandavas sitting there feared it would be all over in a moment, but then Draupadi said, "I'll not mary a charioteer's son". Karna let the bow slip from his grip and retired to his seat.

Finally, Arjuna disguised as Brahman came forward, strung the bow and fixing the arrows shot the target through the hole of the revolving contraption. Draupadi put the garland round his neck and ther was tremendous applause. Soon Arjuna stood before the door of their house and shouted, "Mother, see what alms we have brought". "Share it equally among you all five" returned Kunti from inside, and thus, Draupadi became the common wife of all the five brothers, Soon the true identity of the Pandavas was revealed and they lived happily at Drupada's court as son-in-law. The new that they were alive and had won the princess as bride sent shivers down the spines of the Kauravas. The pandavas were invited to Hastinapur, but Duryodhana was very sour.

Indraprastha

Dhritarashtra welcomed the Pandavas, and in order to pacify them divided the kingdom into two halves, and gave one to the Pandavas. The Pandavas built their magnificent capital called Indraprastha on the banks of the river Yamuna. They had Krishna, Vidura and Drupada as their sincere friends and advisers. One day Narada visited the Pandavas and advised Yudhithira that there should be no dissension among the five brothers on account of the comon wife Draupadi. To be on their guard, they decided that anyone of them who saw a brother making love to Draupadi would be self exiled for 12 years and lead a celibate life.

One day due to some urgency Arjuna had to enter the hall to fetch his weapons, when Yudhisthira and Draupadi were enjoying the privacy. So, Arjuna went into self-exile in spite of Yudhisthira's sincere protests. During the exile he travelled through many lands, and finally came to Dwarka, where Krishna, Arjuna's cousin dwelt. There Arjuna married Subhadra with the help of Krishna and then eloped with her to Indraprastha. Later the marriage was duly solemnized. The pandavas were very happy and well established. Kunti thought gone were the days of suffering and hardship. Draupadi by then had been blessed with five sons, and Subhadra with one, the illustrious Abhimanyu. But it proved like a lull before the storm.

Shishupala slain

The Pandavas grew mightier with the passage of time and decided to perform the Rajasuya Sacrifice at the adivice of rishi Narad. Before beginning the ceremonial sacrifice, they slew the tyrant Jarasandha of Magadha, who had held many princes as prisoners for sacrifice. The great Sacrifice of Rajasuya then began attended by all the kings, rishis, noblemen and others of the land. The coronation ceremony being over, the time to honour the invited guests came, and Krishna was given precedence all over others. But the king of Chedi, Shishupala, a powerful king, objected to it saying that Krishana was a mere cowhed. Shishupala raved in delirium, but Krishna remained cool, collected and smiling as ever. But then Krishna's patience was exhausted. Krishna

69

challenged Shishupala, and a terrible combat began. All the kings stood immobilized at this unexpected turn of events. Krishna took his Sudarshana Chakra (discus), and addressing the august assembly said, "Enough of this nonsense, no more. I am sorry that such an unpleasantness has been created on such a auspicious occasion." Then Krishna chopped off in a flash the head of raving Shishupala with his discus. A light emerged from Shishupala's dead body, made obeisance to Krishna and merged into Krishna. The ceremony being over the princes left for their respective homes.

The Fated Dice and the Stakes

Duryodhana returned from Indraprastha, but his envy of the pandavas became an obsession. With his vile uncle Shakuni, he started scheming and they together plotted the ruin of the pandavas. To deprive the Pandavas of their Kingdom and wealth, Shakuni proposed to challenge Yudhisthira in a game of dice, and the latter had a weakness for the game. The Pandavas were invited to Hastinapur and given a very warm welcome. Shakuni then challenged Yudhisthira to play the game and the latter had to accept it. Shakuni played and Duryodhana provided with the stakes.

The game began in the presence of the august assembly, which included Dhritrashtra, Vidura, Drona and Bhishma. A great excitement prevailed and pearls, jewels, gold, chariots, horses and a lot of wealth was staked, but every time the wicked Shkuni won. Yudhisthira lost all his wealth, kingdom and even his brothers.

Then Shakuni sneered and said, "There is still left Draupadi, the brightest jewel". Yudhisthira put Draupadi on the stake. Shakuni took his turn and exclaimed. "I have won."

The entire assembly was stunned and shocked. Vidura sat with his head between his palms. Bhishma gazed vacantly. The jubilant Duryodhana ordered Draupadi to be fetched there. Vidura asked Duryodhana to see reason and not to do any such foolish thing, but Duryodhana remained adamant. He sent Dushasana to fetch Draupadi.

He approached Draupadi and spoke insolently. Draupadi was scared and ran trembling to the inner quarters. Dushasana chased and brought her dragging to the hall, while Draupadi cried, "Leave me, I am in period, and in a single cloth". But vile Dushasana roughed her saying, "You are now our slave, your husband has lost you in wager. In period, or in single cloth, how does it matter now."

The Pandavas and all the elders looked on helplessly. Draupadi stood outraged and trembling. Dushasana tried to strip her. She looked here and there for help in vain, and then she closed her eyes in prayer. Dushasana went on pulling her clothes and they came off easily, but they had no end, they were getting endless and he had to give up his shameless act.

In her dire distress Draupadi had turned her mind to God, the Lord, protector and the last refuge of destitutes, and her honour was saved in a miraculous way. Mean while, the sinful Duryodhana uncovered his left thigh and showed it to Draupadi, and Bhima vowed, "That is the thigh I will break with my mace. I vow it, if I do not, let perdition be my fate." There were many evil omens seen, and it frightened the blind Dhritrashtra, and he freed the Pandavas and returned to them their kingdom. The Pandavas rode their chariot and departed for Indraprastha in peace.

It mightily displeased Duryodhana, and he insisted on one more game of dice. Dhritrashtra had to agree, and the Pandavas were summoned back when they were on their way to Indraprastha. This time the loser had to go into exile for twelve years, and had to pass the thirteenth incognito. And if discovered during the last year, he had to return to the forest again for twelve years, and again had to pass the thirteen in disguise. It was a strange wager indeed.

Once again they sat down to play, the bet was explained and agreed upon. Once again the dice was cast, and once more Yudhisthira lost and Duryodhana won. The pandavas had to go to the forest in exile as ascetics for twelve years.

Then, Narada appeared and predicted, "Fourteen years from now the kauravas will be annihilated as a result of their sins committed by Duryodhana and his associates". It filled Dhritrashtra and Duryodhana's hearts with terror.

The Pandavas in Exile

The Pandavas walked fast, crossed the rivers Ganga and Yamuna, and reached the Kamyaka forest. Learning of there exile, king Drupada came running to see them, and so came Krishna. Draupadi narrated in sobbes how she was outraged and molested in the assembly. Krishana comforted and told her, "Draupadi, your tears will be suitably avenged, and then the ladies of Kuru will wail and weep even as you are doing now take my word". Dhrishtadyumna, Draupadi's brother also vowed to avenge all the wrongs done to the Pandavas. The Pandavas travelled across many lands contemplating how to avenge the wrongs upon the wicked Kauravas.

Meanwhile, Arjuna practised severe penance in the Himalayas and obtained many celestial weapons from Lord Shiva. Yudhisthira along with Drupadi and three younger brothers travelled throughout the length and breadth of the country, made pilgrimage and earned religious and spiritual merits. During their exile, the Pandavas led an adventurous life and performed many heroic and wonderful feasts. Thus, they spent the twelve years of their exile. When the thirteenth year, which they had to spend incognito, approached, they set out for Matsya, the kingdom of good king Virata. The Pandavas disguised themselves into different persons. Yudhisthira became Kanka, the companion of the king in the game of dice. Bhima the king's cook, Arjuna a eunuch to serve the royal ladies, Nakula the keeper of the royal horses,and Sahadeva the keeper of the cows and the bulls. Draupadi choose the role of the personal serving maid of the queen Sudeshana.

Soon the last year of their exile, the thirteenth year of incognito living was over, and their true identities were revealed. The king of Virata offered his daughter Uttara to Abhimanyu for the Pandavas had protected his kingdom from a fierce attack of the Kauravas. The wedding celebrations being over, the question of restoring the kingdom of Indraprastha to the Pandavas was debated upon. Krishna, Balram, Satyki and Drupada were the chief speakers. It was decided that the issue be settled by peaceful and honourable means. but if it failed war was to be resorted.

The War Preparations

Drupada sent an envoy to Dhritrashtra on behalf of the Pandavas to make the Kauravas agree to render the kingdom back to the Pandavas. But the willful Duryodhana did not agree to return the kingdom. Krishna visited Hastinapur to settle the matter amicably, but again Duryodhana refused to see reason and make peace with his cousins. Krishna said, "Duryodhana, if you do not return to your cousins their kingdom, give them at least five villages and they will be contented". The evil Duryodhana remained adamant and replied, "They will not have even as much as the needle-point of the land" and beside rage he left the hall. With him went out Karna, Shakuni and Dushasana.

Krishna failed in his peace mission and the war became inevitable. Krishna met Karna in a secluded place and revealed him his birth and parentage. He appealed Karna to accept Kunti his mother and the Pandavas as his younger brothers. But Karna remained steadfast like a rock in his loyalty to his dear friend Duryodhana. Neither fear of death, nor the temptation of crown; however strong, could swerve him from his path of duty and righteousness. Krishna embraced Karna, pressed his hand in affection and went away.

It made Kunti most unhappy. She went alone to see his eldest son Karna on the banks of the Ganga, where Karna practised tapas everyday in the morning. She appealed to Karna to be united with his younger brothers, but he refused to be untrue to his salt, however, he granted a boon to Kunti and promised to spare the lives of four of the Pandavas, except that of Arjuna. Kunti wept and sobbed and then they parted.

The hectic war preparations began and soon reached their heights. Kings and princes began to assemble with their armies. Many of them had common blood relations with the Kauravas and the Pandavas, and it became difficult for them to decide in favour of the either. Krishna had already decided in favour of the Pandavas, but Balarama remained neutral. The armies began to pour in the famous plains of Kurukshetra. Tents were being erected, chariots rumbled, elephants trumpeted, horses neighed, conches blew, soldiers shouted slapping their armpits and the sky rent with the great pandemonium. Both the armies stood facing each other, and looked like two agitated seas at the time of Dissolution. Bhishma led the Kaurava army, but on the condition that he would destroy the Pandava army, but not the Pandavas, and that either he or Karna would fight, not the both together.

Cut to the quick, Karna refused to fight till Bhishma was there. The battle was about to begin when Arjuna, overwhelmed with pity and sorrow, dropped his bow Gandiva and arrows, and slumped down on his seat in the chariot. Krishna then enlightend Arjuna with that transcendental knowledge known as "Bhagavad Gita", under lining the fact the one's duty or dharma is of the supreme importance. At last Arjuna's delusion disappeared by Krishna's grace, and he took up Gandiva and was ready to fight.

The Battle Begins

The battle began with a great tumult rending the air. Arrows spread in all directions like shooting stars. Bhishma was the supreme commander of the Kaurava forces. He penetrated the Pandava defences and carried doom and destruction with him. Abhimanyu rallied the Pandava forces, helped by Bhima, Virata and others. Uttara clashed with great Salya but was slain by the latter. The initial defeat and setback made the Pandava generals wiser, and on the second day Dhrishtadyumna arrayed the forces with great care. Arjuna engaged Bhishma in a fierce battle. The fight was well and equally balanced. At another place Drona and Drupada fought a fierce dual.

Day after day passed by, and it was the ninth day of the battle. Bhima, in his full fury, mowed down the enemy. His son Ghatkacha defeated and disgraced Duryodhana. The enemy forced ran pell-mell before Bhishma's attack and the Pandava host was once again completely demoralised. Bhishma appeared like the god of Death itself in his blazing armour, and it became clear that as long Bhishma was there, the Pandavas themselves would not be victorious. On the tenth day Krishna urged Arjuna to kill Bhishma at the very first opportunity. Bhishma began his work of devastation. Then came Arjuna, keeping Shikhandin before him as protection. Arjuna shot deadly arrows from behind Shikhandin, and Bhishma stood silent and smiling. Finally Bhishma fell down pierced and bristled with hundreds of arrows, and the battle stopped for the day.

Shikhandin was a girl by birth, but later changed into a man by virtue of a boon granted in the previous birth. Therefore, Bhishma would not shoot at Shikhandin, he being a woman by birth, Arjuna took advantage of it, and sheltering behind Shikhandin, fatally wounded Bhishma. Pierced all over by Arjuna's sharp darts, Bhishma fell down, but his body touched not the ground.

The Great Drona

After Bhishma's fall, Drone was made the commander of the Kaurava forces. It was the eleventh day of the great battle. The battle resumed and the combats began. Drona's sharp arrows cleaved apart the enemy defences. Drona wanted to take Yudhisthira a captive, but Arjuna's fierce fight made Drona beat a retreat. The second day of Drona's leadership dawned and the battle began anew. On the third day's battle. Abhimanyu was the hero. It was he who successfully pentrated the Chakravyuha formation of the enemy forces, and died fighting fiercely single handed the combined attack of Kama, Shakuni, Salya, Aswathama and others. The next day, Arjuna consumed with the thought of avenging Abhimanyu, cut his way through the thick enemy formations and killed Jayadratha. The war went on, and so the holocaust continued, even through the night. Drona consumed the enemy like conflagration. But then the Pandavas managed to slay him by telling a lie that his son Aswathama had been killed. Bhima killed an elephant of the same name and then declared Ashwathama was killed. When Drone asked Yudhisthira, "Is my son Aswathama truly slain!" Yudhisthira replied, "Yes, Aswathama is dead" and softly added, "the elephant". the latter words were completely drowned in the clamour and not heard by Drona.

Hearing of his son's death, Drona lost interest in the fight. he dropped his weapons and sat down in meditation. Then Dhrishtadyumna rushed and cut off his head.

Karna Commands the Hosts

Fifteen days of war had gone by, and on the sixteenth day, after Drona's death, the Kaurvas anointed Kama their commander, the third in succession. The armies clashed again and single combats and duels resumed. Before the fire of the Kama's fiery attack the enemy forces melted, and dared not to withstand him. The fight continued well past sunset, but then the cease was announced.

On the second day of his command, Radheya came determined to defeat the Pandavas once for all. Yudhisthira challenged Karna and a terrible battle unsued. Finally, Karna made Yudhisthira defenceless with his furious attacks, but spared his life. Karna pressed forward and soon stood in front of Arjuna's car. The fierce duel began, which was well balanced and equally matched. Suddenly the left wheel of Karna's chariot got stuck in the bloody mud, Karna jumped down and bent to lift up the wheel. But then Arjuna shot a fatal arrow and severed defenceless karna's head from his body.

Karna's death plunged Duryodhana in an ocean of abysmal sorrow. He saw despair and destruction all around. He consulted his remaining friends and heroes and made Salya, the king of Madra, their commander. Salya arranged his handful of forces into a clever battle formation, and the eighteenth day of the great battle began with fierce fighting. Salya wrought havoc with his boundless might. It made Yudhisthira angry. He could not any longer tolerate the wholesale massacre of his forces. He fought like the god of Death himself, and slew Salya with a terrible dart. Thus, the great war was almost over. Duryodhana, wounded and weeping, fled, and hid himself under the water of a lake. He solidified the water and lay down hidden from the view. But soon he was discovered by the Pandavas. A terrible mace duel was fought between Duryodhana and Bhima, but finally Bhima broke Duryodhana's thighs with a couple of mighty strokes, and he fell down fatally wounded and died later. The Pandavas shouted for joy, and in victory.

Now, the Pandavas were soverigns. The coronation of Yudhisthira was duly solemnized, and he ruled over the vast kingdom, but he was not happy at all. The Pandavas performed the great Horse-sacrfice. Soon after the sacrifice Krishna and Balrama passed away. Their passing away was the greatest blow to the Pandavas. Life had lost its meaning to them. They knew their time of departure had come. They crowned their grandson Parikshita and set out on their last and great pilgrimage to the Himalayas.

The Bhagvad Gita

Inset in the Mahabharata, the Bhagvad Gita, popularly known simply as the Gita, is an integral part of the epic, nay the quintessence. It is in a dialogue form between Arjuna and Krishna. Arjuna enquires and Krishna answers. It reflects intimacy, informality and friendliness, the charms of a conversation, and yet it is highly serious, sublime and subtle. Upanishadic in nature, it bears close resemblance to many Upanishads, particularly to the Svetashvatara Upanishad, for they both aim at the synthesis of theism and monism and such other trends. It is a great religio-philosophic, work which reconciles different paths of salvation. It shows different paths, but never under estimates the one in favour of the other, though it may underline the one as more suited and easy for a person with a particular bent of mind and temperament.

It is a unique gospel on Karma-yoga, and teaches how to attain the great ideal of worklessness through work. Renunciation of the fruits of action is the ideal suggested in the Gita. Man should not renounce the work and social responsibilities, but fruits thereof. In other words one should work without any attachment to the work and hope of its fruits. It is the attachment which leads to suffering and bondage. Attachment and desires are the root of evil. It is by following Svadharma or one's assigned duties that one can attain God. When Arjuna, in the battlefield of Kurukshetra, succumbs to despondency and shrinks from his duty as a warrior and Kshatriya, because of his attachment to his kinsmen, teachers, fathers, sons, uncles, father-in-law and others, Shri Krishna urges him to fight with his mind ever fixed on the Lord. Arjuna is a prince and a Kshatriya. It is his duty to fight the unrighteous Kauravas. He should not try to escape his svadharma. If Arjuna thinks that he will not fight, it is a vain resolve, his very nature will compel him to act, however, he can be free from the binding results of his action by undertaking if selflessly, dedicating its fruits at the feet of the Lord :

"Seek to perform your duty, but claim not
to reap the fruits of your action.
Do not seek the rewards of what you do
neither shall you be inactive.
Being fixed in Yoga, perform your duty
renouncing attachment, be indifferent
both to success and failure.
Equilibrium is verily yoga.
O Dhananjaya, motivated karma is inferior,

77

to that done in equnimity of mind,

taking refuge in the evenness of mind.

Harassed are the seekers of fruits".

–Bhagvad Gita II, 47-49

Lord Krishna preaches that sorrows and sufferings can be overcome by equnimity of mind and sense of proportion which amount to real detachment. The problem here with Arjuna is that his approach is egoistic. He considers himself the doer of the act, and not the nimitta or the willing instrument in the hands of God. This marks the real difference between nishkama karma and sakama karma. A nishkama karma is essentially non-egoistic and objective, performed for the wellbeing of both the doer and the others. In such an action man feels that he is not the actual doer or the agent of the action, but a mere instrument, a means in the hands of God. This is also called karma-sanyasa or renunciation of work. When a work is performed non-egoistically without hankering after the fruits of it, without any sense of attachment, such a work becomes nishkama or desireless work. Fruits there are, but they are offered at the feet of the Lord. A work done with desire and attachment leads to bondage, while a desireless work paves the path to liberation. One is born out of ignorance, the other out of knowledge. Actions are natural to man; cessation of work is an impossibility. Therefore, Krishna teaches that our actions should be Satvika, that is done with mental equipoise in a spirit of detachment according to our dharma and duty. Inaction or passivity is totally undesirable because it is Tamasika and has its roots in nescience. The desireless and detached deeds constitute the karmayoga. But it never means performing a work mechanically without taking into consideration its consequences. An enlightened person should also perform a work with the same zest as would an ignorant man with an eye on the reward, but without any hankering after the fruit. In modern times Mahatma Gandhi has been one of the greatest examples of Karma Yogis.

Arjuna shrinks from fighting and his limbs fail under the delusion that it would involve him in violence and sin. Then enlightening him, Lord Krishna says that it is the body that gets destroyed and not the soul. "Weapons do not harm the Atman, fire burns it not, water wets it not, wind dries it not. Atman cannot be cleaved, kindled, wetted or dried. It is eternal all-pervading, immovable and stable". In the light of this knowledge, Arjuna is made ready to fight in an altogether different frame of mind, which does not entail any bondage or sin at all. It is the equimindedness which renders a man immune and indifferent both to success and failure. Arjuna is urged to perform his duty without malice, illwill or desire for fruits. It is this attitude which transforms an action into a Sattvika and Nrivatti karma. It is the spirit and the attitude which matters the most. Thus, nishkama karma bolds the greatest hope for all the men of action.

CHAPTER FOUR

Pantheism and Polytheism

Hinduism is monistic and monotheistic in essence, but this essence often gets undermined by its apparent pantheism, polytheism and rich mythology. Hinduism at popular levels is pantheistic and henotheistic. With the passage of time many gods and goddesses of Vedic period were relegated to a secondary position in popular HInduism, and many new ones came into existence. This plathora of deities of the Hindu pantheon, can be called a tribute to its rich imaginative and assimilative genius, but at the same time it also reflects its weakness, in the sense that in the multiplicity of gods and goddesses its true spirit of oneness of Reality is lost sight of. Popular Hinduism seems to emphasize immanance of Brahmana at the expanse of its transcendence. In the Vedic pantheon there were very many deities like Indra, Agni, Varuna, Mitra, Usha, Maruts, Ashvins, Rudra and others.

Hinduism finds the manifestation of divinity in pracitcally everything, specially in things which uphold, sustain and nourish life. For example, many manifestations of nature and its power like fire, wine and the sun personified as Agni, Marut and Surya respectively are held in high regard as gods because of the belief that they sustain and nourish life, and the succession of seasons, etc., is due to their powers. In the Vedas many collection of hymns are dedicated to these gods and goddesses. Many deities who earlier represented the various aspects of nature came to possess elaborate mythology which enthropomorphised them.

HINDU TRINITY

The Hindu Trinity of Brahma, Vishnu and Shiva or Mahesha marks the beginning of an epoch in the Hinduism. Later it gave rise to distinct and main streams of Hinduism, namely, Vaishnavism and Shaivism about the first century before the beginning of the Christian era. The trinity represents the creative, preservative and destructive aspects and three gunas (strands): rajas, sattava and tamas respectively. It also represents an attempt to reconcile and synthesise the two main directions of Vaishnavism and Shaivism. The Vedas foreshadows the Trinity. Brahma owes its origin to the Vedic concept of Prajapati, the creator. Brahma has no cult, no temples and worshippers simply because as a creator he has no direct bearing on the personal lives of the Hindus. As a creator he has set in motion the abstract principles by which the entire creation operates. These laws of operation, already in force, are eternal and unchangeable. Hence, Brahma is seldom worhsipped as a god and has no followers.

BRAHMA

Brahma is represented with four faces and four hands and a blowing beard, as a grand old and wise god. In one hand he holds a conch shell, a rosary in another, a water jug in the third and the Veda in the fourth. Saraswati, the goddess of learning is his consort and Hansa, the swan is his mount. He created this universe and every cycle of creation lasts one of Brahma's days which is equivalent to 2, 160, 000, 000 years. At the end of such a cycle this whole universe, including Brahma himself, is dissolved, and it is called Mahapralaya or Great Dissolution. Then another Brahma is born and a new cycle begins. The cycle is divided into sub-cycles, known as Kalpas. An imortant sub-division of Kalpa is Mahayuga, and each Mahayuga consists of four Yugas, namely, Krita Yuga, Treta Yuga, Dwapara Yuga and Kali Yuga. The first one is a golden age and lasts for 1, 728, 000 years. Treta is a silver age and lasts for 1, 296, 000 years. The Dwapara, which lasts for 864, 000 years, is a copper age. The Kali Yuga or the iron age is the worst and marks the degeneration in human values and dharma. It lasts for 432, 000 years. During dissolution gods, men and Brahma mege into Brahman, the first cause. Every dissolution thus coincides with Brahma's life. Brahma is shown to have been born from a lotus springing from Vishnu's navel, or to have hatched out from the golden cosmic egg floating on the cosmic waters.

VISHNU

The Vishnu second of the Hindu triad, Vishnu represents the

preservative aspect. As a preserver he is the embodiment of sattava guna and the upholder of righteousness and dharma. In his anthropomorphic representation, Vishnu is a handsome youth with blue skin and all the marks of royalty. He as four hands; one holds a conch shell, the second a chakra or discus, the third a mace and the fourth a lotus flower. Lakshmi, the goddess of wealth is his consort and Garuda, half-man and half-bird, his vehicle. Vishnu is also shown reclining on the bed of the serpent Sheshanaga, with Lakshmi or Sri seated at his feet. Vaikuntha is his heaven and is built entirely of gold and jewels. There in the pools grow white, red and blue lotuses. The Ganga is said to have originated from his foot.

Vishnu is a very popular deity and is worshipped throughout the Hindu world and has thousand names, the repetition of which removes sins and bestows religious merits and bliss. He has a bow called Saranga and a sword called Nandaka. The devotees of Vishnu recognise him as the supreme being, the source of all creation.

Vishnu is there as a god in the Vedas, but is role as a great preserver is a development of later times. In the Rigveda, he represents the solar energy and is shown striding over the entire universe in three steps—

"Three times strode forth this God in all

his grandeur over this earth bright with

a hundred splendours.

Foremost be Vishnu, stronger than the strongest,

for glorious is his name who lives for ever.

Over this earth with mighty step strode

Vishnu, ready to give it for a home to Manu.

In him the humble people trust for safety,

he, nobly born, hath made them spacious

dwellings".

—The Rigveda, C, 3-4

With the passage of time, Vishnu acquired new powers and attributes, and new legends and mythology grew around him till he becomes the second of the Hindu Triad in the Puranic age. As such, he is associated with grace, mercy, all-pervasiveness and the watery element, which spreads everywhere before the creation of the world. In this form he is Nara, the cosmic ocean. He is also called Narayana, "moving in the waters", and is represented reclining on the serpent Shesha and floating on the waters. A divine lotus is shown growing from his navel as he slumbers, and Brahma arising from that lotus. This posture is resumed by Vishnu after each dissolution. In the Mahanarayana Upanishad he has been described as Supreme Being with his cosmic character.

SHIVA

Shiva or Mahesha, the third of the Hindu Trimurti is another popular deity. Rudra is another name of Shiva, and Rudra is one of the Vedic gods. There he is praised as "the lord of the songs, the lord of sacrifices, who heals, is brilliant as the sun, the best and most bountiful of gods:". In the Yajurveda he has been described as "auspicious not terrible", "the deliverer, the first divine physician", he is "blue-necked and red coloured, who has a thousand eyes and bears a thousand quivers", and in another mantra he is called "Trumbaka, the sweet-scented increaser of prosperity". In the Atharvaveda he is the lord of the beasts, but he is fiercer. In the Upanishads and the epics he holds a very high position as the Supreme Being and a pesonal god respectively. The rival claims of Vishnu and Shiva to supremacy and reconciled in the concept of the Hindu Triad. Shiva symbolises the principle of annihilation, and dissolution, but in fact his attributes and powers are much more numerous and wider. Shankara, Mahadeva, Maheshwara, Bhava, Sarva, Pashupati Tryambaka are some of his other names. Parvati is his consort and Nandi the bull, his mount. As Pashupati he is the lord of the beasts and cattle.

In his creative aspect he is Mahadeva, Ishvara, the Supreme Lord. His supreme creative powers are worshipped in the form of the lingam or phallus, of all the divine expressions, the Lingam can be said to be most representative of the powers of regeneration and procreation. The Lingam coupled with the Yoni, the symbol of female life-force, or the female organ, he is worshipped everywhere. There is hardly any place of worship where a Lingam is not found. Regeneration and dissolution are the two aspects of the same coin. One presupposes the other. As a Maha-kala he is a great destroying and dissolving force. As a Mahayogi, he is constantly absorbed in severe austerities and derives his powers from them. He is naked, Digambara (sky-clad) and his body is smeared with ashes. He is also the lord of the ghosts, witches, dwarfs and goblins and is Bhuteshwara. In these forms and aspects he haunts the cemeteries, cremation grounds wearing serpents round his head and arms and a garland of skulls. Besides Lingam, he is also worshipped as an anthroponeophic god. Shiva is a complex and multi-dimensional deity and is represented doing several roles, both good and evil, in this great drama of regeneration and dissolution. He is Nilkantha or blue-throated because during the churning of the ocean for amrit, he swallowed the poison and rendered a vital service to the gods. As Nataraj, he is the lord of the dance and drama. By Tandava he accomplished the dissolution of the world. Shiva's dance stands both for his glory and rhythm of life and the universe. He carries a trident and is generally accompanied by his Nandi bull. His abode is on Mount Kailasa. He is also shown with a third eye in the centre of his forehead, which is very destructive. With it, he once reduced Kamadeva the god of love, because Kamadeva tried to excite him sexually while he was engaged in a great penance. In Shaivism, Shiva is worshipped as the Supreme personal God. Shaivism combines the Aryan and non-Aryan religious beliefs and ideas. he is father of gods Genesh and Kartikeya.

AVATARS

The concept of Avatars (Incarnations) or Descents is found in the Vedas in a seed form. There we find the definite though faint indications of the descent of Vishnu on the earth in human form in order to accomplish certain objectives. The circumstances which necessitate the descent of Vishnu is described in these lines of the Gita—

Whenever Dharma declines, and
Unrighteousness flourishes then I incarnate
Myself, O Bharata.
I incarnate age after age,
for the protection of the good, and
for the destruction of the wicked, and
for-re-establishment of Dharma

—The Bhagvad Gita, IV 7-8

In the Puranas various legends are give as regard to the Avatars of Vishnu. His various incarnations, right from in the form of a fish (Matsya) through tortoise (Kurma), boar (Varaha, man-lion) Narsimha), dwarf (Vamana), Parshurama, Rama and Krishna, symbolically represent the evolution of life and society. An avtar is an embodied portion of Vishnu's divine essence in a human or supernatural form. By coming down on the earth as an Avatar, Vishnu as a preserver, performs the specific task of destroying the evil-doers and establishing and preserving the rule of dharma. In all there are ten Avatars, but the seventh and the eighth, Rama and Krishna are held in great awe and reverence and receive worship as great gods. As we have already seen, Rama is the hero of the beautiful epic poem, the Ramayana of Valmiki. Krishna is the great hero of many legends and myths. In the Mahabharata he delivers the famous song, the Bhagved Gita to Arjuna as the manifestation of the Supreme Being. His supreme divinity further finds expression in Bhagavata Purana and Harivansa. He killed many demons, asuras and tyrants including pralamba, Kansa, Jarasandha and Shishupala.

BUDDHA

Gautam Buddha is regarded as the ninth incarnation of Vishnu. It is believed that Vishnu appeared as Buddha not as a hero-upholder of dharma and righteousness, but to encourage the wicked and demonic to despise Vedas, reject cast, and deny the existence of God, and thus causing them their own destruction. The inclusion of Buddha as an avatar in the Hindu pantheon underlines the great power of assimilation and absorption of other cults and creeds into itself. In the Bhagavad Gita Lord Krishna says, "Even those who worship other gods with devotion, worship me alone, O sonof kunti, though but by the worng method" (IX, 23). This utterance of Krishna points out how Hinduism can incorporate into itself other gods and goddesses by regarding them as the manifestations of the same Supreme Beings. Buddha himself was brought up, lived and died as a Hindu, Buddhism owes much to Hinduism. But then Hinduism was much enriched by Buddhist moral Philosophy.

The tenth incarnation of Vishnu Kalki is yet to descend at the end of the present age Kali Yuga, with a drawn sword blazing like lightning and seated on a white borse. He will accomplish the final ruin of the wicked and prepare the ground for the renovation of creation, and the restoration of dharma and purity.

MOTHER GODDESS

The three great gods of the Hindu Trinity have their respective female counter-parts and spouses. These goddesses who complement their husbands are popular deities of the, Hindu pantheon. Uma or Parvati is the consort of Shiva, and is the most popular of the three being the Mother Goddess. Saraswati the goddess of learning is the consort of Brahma and Lakshmi, the goddess of wealth that of Vishnu. The history and origin of Uma as mother goddess goes back to Harappan period, where many statuettes of nude female symbolising yoni and fertility have been found along with the horned god figuirines with exposed male organ, identified as Proto-Shiva. It seems that Linga-worship and the cult of Mother Goddess was in vogue in the Harappan civilization. Thus both Shiva and Durga are pre-Vedic and non-Aryan deities which later found their way into the Hindu pentheon.

UMA

Uma is Saharsaranana or thousand-named, which represent her various aspects both fierce and beneficent. Like Shiva himself, she is the mistress of several attributes and powers and reflects a complex and multidimensional personality. Among the goddesses Uma is the only one who has so distinct personality, her family and a group of interesting legends and myths. She is Ambiku (mother), Mahamaya (great illusion), Durga (inaccessible), Shakti (female energy), Devi (goddess), Sarva-mangala (ever auspicious), Kamakshi (wanton-eyed), Kali (black), etc. She is the daughter of Himalaya mountains, and Shakti of female energy of Shiva. She is both fierce and benevolent. In her mild and kind aspect, she is the giver of life and in her fierce and terrifying aspect, she destroys in the form of pestilence, disease and famine. As a creative and life-force, she helps Shiva in creation and greneration; without her motivating life-force no creation is possible for Shiva. It implies that no creativity, whether spiritual or physical, is possible without the union of the opposing forces. She represents the female principle and Shiva the male principle. As Sati she is the daughter of Daksha. As Chandi (fierce) she receives blood sacrifices. As Durga she rides a tiger in a fierce mood and carries

Lord Vishnuji

Lord Vishnu — the Preserver sometimes represented as dark complexioned usually holds in his four hands a Padma (lotus), a Gada (mace), a Shanka (conch), and a Chakra (discus).

weapons in all her ten hands. As Kali, she is shown with a terrible countenance. In both these aspects, she is single without a spouse. As Durga and Kali she is a goddess complete in herself, representation of all the forms and forces that destroy evil and promote good and well-being of the world.

LAKSHMI

The next in importance is Lakshmi, the consort of Vishnu. Her origin and history cannot be traced either in the Indus Valley religion or the Vedic literature. Thus, she seems to be of puranic origin. She is a goddess of good fortune, wealth, abundance, agriculture, and trade and commerce, and she has her own personality and traits. But as a wife of Vishnu, she does not possess much independent and powerful personality as does Uma. For the most part she is seen at Vishnu's side as an appendage and adornment of her lord. Lakshmi or sri's origin is related with the churning of the milky ocean. At the time of the churning of the Ocean, she sprang from the occan's foam, like Aphrodite, on Vishnu's chest which is her proper place, in her full splendour and beauty with a lotus bloom in her hand. Another myth represents her as floating on the lotus flower at the time of creation. Therefore, she is also called Padma (lotus).

When Vishnu incarnates himself as Rama, she descended as Sita, and when Vishnu was born as Krishna, she became Radha. Lakshmi as Sita supports her consort Vishnu in his struggle and triumph over evil and adharma. Lakshmi as Radha again symbolises the union of opposites which is the basis of all creation. Lakshmi and Vishnu represent the concept of unity in diversity. In latent form the Reality is one, but when manifested, it becomes many. Lakshmi can also be identified as Prakriti or Maya of the Purusha. Lakshmi is represented with four hands. She does not have temples dedicated to herself, but as a companion and consort of Narain. There are temples and temples called "Lakshmi-Narain"shrines, where Vishnu and Lakshmi are installed together as wife and husband.

SARASVATI

Sarasvati, the wife of Brahma, is the goddess of learning and speech. She is both a goddess and a river, now lost. As a river-goddess also she is still worshipped and invoked. She is the inventress of the Sanskrit language and Devnagari script, and the patroners of various arts and sciences. She is prayed to and worshipped for acquiring knowledge and wisdom. She is always shown seated on a lotus flower and playing a veena. The white peocock or a white swan is her vehicle. Her graceful figure is ever depicted dressed in spotless white, and except a garland of white flowers, she does not wear any other jewellery. She is the mother of the Vedas which sprang from her head. According to another legend Sarasvati was originally the wife of Vishnu, along with Lakshmi and Ganga, but as they used to quarrel among themselves, Vishnu gave Sarasvati to Brahma and Ganga to Shiva.

The corresponding triad of goddess Sarasvati, Lakshmi and Parvati are said to have been originally one goddess. Once Vishnu, Brahma and Shiva were confronted with a problem of slaying asura Andhaka, who had a thousand arms and heads and two thousand eyes and feet. As the three gods sat discussing and their glances met, a combined energy in a female form was produced. It dazzled the heavens with its brilliance and was of white red and black colours. As each of these gods wanted to possess this goddess she divided herself into three forms of sarasvati, Lakshmi and Parvati. Thus, they are sisters and have a common origin, but they are mutually incompatible, specially Sarasvati and Lakshmi. That is why a man can have either knowledge and learning or wealth, but not both.

GANESHA

The elephant-headed god Ganesh, the Lord of the Ganas, is one of the most popular Hindu deities. The son of Parvati and Shiva, Ganesha is the god of wisdom, success and good luck. He is worshipped at the beginning of every good work, so that it may be successful and there are no obstacles in the way. He is a great remover of obstacles. He is very wise, learned and a good scribe, and is said to have written down the Mahabharata from the dictation of Vyasa. As Ganapati, he is the lord of Ganas or Shiva's hosts. He is gentle and friendly and bestows success.

He is represented as a portly man with an elephant's head and four hands. In one hand he holds a conch shell, in another a discus, in the third a goad and in the fourth a water lily. The mouse is his Vehicle and

Lord Shivji

Lord Shiva — represents the complete cyclic process of generation,
destruction and regeneration. The all embracing nature of Lord Shiva
is reflected in his 1008 names.

he is shown riding a rat or attended by one. It is very interesting to know how he came to possess his elephant head.

One version has it that once Parvati went to her bath and asked his son to keep watch at the door. Then came Shiva and wanted to enter and was opposed, so he enraged severed the head from his body. To pacify Parvati he replaced it with an elephant's, the first that came to sight.

Yet another legend says that Parvati proud of her son, asked and insisted Shani (Saturn) to look at him forgetting the ruinous effects of Shani's glance. No sooner did he look then Ganesha's head was burnt to ashes. Parvati grew furious and cursed Shani for killing her son, but then Brahma intervented and told her that if the first available head was put on Ganesha's trunk he would be restored to life. To first that could be found was that of an elephant.

Ganesha is worshipped universally throughout the Hindu world, and it precedes all other rituals. There is a legend which explains the reason of this precedence. Once Shiva and Parvati were sitting along with their sons Ganesha and Kartikeya. Then, Shiva Proposed to see who of his two sons came back first, after circling round the world. Kartikeya immediately hurried of mounting his vehicle, the peacock. Meanwhile Ganesha took round of his parents and stood before them with joined palms, saying, "you both are my whole world". It immediately pleased Shiva and Parvati. They blessed him profusely and gave him the boon of being prayed to and worshipped before any auspicious work was begun. Gajanana, Ganapati, Lambodara and Vighnesha are his other popular names. Siddhi and Buddhi are his two wives and Kartikeya his brother.

KARTIKEYA

Kartikeya, the chief war god of the Hindu Pantheon, is also known as Skanda and Kumara. Once Fire or Agni received Shiva's seed, which was afterwards transferred to Ganga, and Kumara was the result. He was brought up by the planet Kritikas (Pliades), and so has six heads and is called Kartikeya. He has six pairs of arms and legs, and carries a bow and an arrow. Peacock is his vehicle. As a commander of the forces of the gods, he is interested only in military exploits and is called Kumara (bachelor), because he is not interested in women at all.

But according to another legend he is the husband of Devasena, an anthromorphic representation of the army of gods. In south India he is known as Subramaniya. He was born with the specific purpose of destrouing a powerful demon, Taraka, whose serve penance had made him invincible to the other gods.

HANUMAN

The monkey-god Hanuman is another very popular deity. He is the embodiment of the Hindu ideal of perfect service, wisdom, speed and strength. He was born of a monkey queen known as Anjana and the Windgod Vayu. Anjana was apsara who was transformed into a monkey under a curse. As soon as he was born he leapt at the sun taking it to be fruit and wanted to satisfy his hunger. Indra saw it and to save the sun, he struck Hanuman with his thunderbolt, and he fell down on the earth. It enraged Vayu and he stopped blowing , causing great discomfort to all the beings. Indra humbly apologised to Vayu and granted Hanuman the boon of great strength and immortality. But his immortality and perpetual youth are considered more often as a gift from Rama.

Hanuman is a great hero in the Ramayana. There are described his exploits and adventures in great detail. He along with other monkeys helped Rama against the demon king Ravana. In one bound he crossed the sea and reached Lanka in search of Sita. As a punishment his tail was set on fire by Ravana, but he with it caused havoc and conflagration in Lanka. His services to Rama were great and many. He killed many Rakshasha-chiefs, flew to the Himalayas to fetch the medicinal herbs to restore Lakshmana to life.

His form is enormous and complexion golden. His face is like bright ruby and his mighty tail spreads out to a great length. Generally he is shown bearing a mace in his hand or sitting with folded hands before Rama and Sita. Through him is expressed the highest divinely in animal form. He is prayed daily by the devout Hindus for strength, well-being and protection against evil forces and ghosts. As such , he is called Sankata-Mochana or deliverer from the troubles.

Among the lesser gods of present Hindu pantheon may be included Kubera, Yama, Indra, Kamdeva, etc. Indra was the most powerful Vedic war-god, but now he holds a subordinate position as the guardian of estern quarter of the universe. Yama, the god of death and guardian of the nothern quarter, dwells in Alkapuri, Veruna is another Lokpala and guards the western quarter of the Universe Kamdeva, the god of love (Eros) is a Vedic god, but he represents not merely the urge of sexual enjoyment, but all the desires and actions in common for the general good. He is the first desire that satisfies allother subsequent desires. Rati, the goddess of desire is his wife. Then there are local village gods and goddesses which include Bhairava, often identified with Shiva, Shitala, the goddess of small pox, Hoimatea, Santoshimata, Mansa, the snake goddess and others. The Grahas or the heavenly objects like the Sun, Moon, Mars, Mercury, Venus, Saturn, Jupiter, Rahu and Ketu, the planets of the solar system are also considered divine and worshipped. Out of the planets, the Sun, the Moon and Saturn (Shani) are worshipped on their own right, but others may be worshipped, if they have malefic and adverse effect on the individual according to his horoscope. Graha actually means the power that seizes and obscures an individual's personality. As such, the evil spirits, with which people, especially children and women are possessed, and which are supposed to cause death, sickness and madness, are worshipped and offered sacrifices for propitiation.

The legendary rishis, munis and sages of old, who achieved divinity by their meritorious acts, are held in great reverence and offered worship. The "Saptarishis" identified with stars of the constellation Great Bear and Narada, Vyasa, Valmiki, Vashishtha, Gautama, etc. come under this category. They acquired a state of godhood and divinity by their severe penances and other sacrifices. The living sages and saints are also worshipped as they posses divine powers capable of influencing men's lives and fortunes. Hindu divinity is all-inclusive and in a way, extends to the whole creation. Saints, sages and holy personages are help in reverence during their life and after their death, because divinity found expression through them to lesser or greater extent. The more the expression of divinity through a man, the greater the reverence he is help in. Besides the cow, tulsi (basil) plant, asavatha (peepal), bada (banayan) trees are sacred to the Hindus. Certain lakes, rivers and water are holy and sacred, and as such they are often given anthropomorphic forms and offered worship and propitiation. Among the rivers the Ganga and the Yamuna are the most sacred. Among the lakes the one at Pushkar near Ajmer and the other Mansarovar, near Mount Kailash in the Himalayas are held in great reverence.

Obviously, the Hindu pantheon in quite large and rich. In Vedic times religion was in the form of nature-worship. Then there were neither temples nor idols. In this religion the elements and various power of nature were personified and worshipped. The concept of divinity in Hinduism is based on the principle that divine beings gods and object uphold the universe together physically and morally, and prevent the occurrence of any kind of chaos and disorder. They are good and righteous and maintain dharma. The world owes its origin and continuation to them. Therefore, they are worshipworthy and their relation with mankind is so intimate and friendly. For example, Varuna, as the creator of the physical and moral laws according to the Rita or cosmic order, and their maintainer, was prayed for forgiveness of sins arising out of the violation of the laws. The cosmic laws are inviolable and binding on both gods and men. Similarly, Indra, the thunder-god helped his devotees in the war against the hostile people, and also by liberating the waters by slaying the demons of draught. So Indra, the rain-god became the national god of the Vedic Aryans.

The early Aryans worshipped and offered oblations to various gods and goddesses such as Varuna, Indra, Surya, Vayu, Agni, Aditi, Usha, Soma, Rudra, and Vishnu for abundant crops, for obtaining milch-kine, steeds and cattle, progenies, happiness here and bliss in heaven. They also prayed for long life of hundred years and for destroying the enemy. They belived that heaven was a post-mortem existence full of effulgene, complete satisfaction, joy and happiness. But gradually the idea of obtaining heavenly abode, as the highest goal of life, was replaced by the concept of moksha or final liberation. But porpitiation of gods through ritual sacrifice and attainment of heaven as a reward still remained an ideeal on popular levels, and a particular god continued to receive worship and was lauded as the supreme being in a particular collection of hymns, though other deities were not denied. Many gods represented the same natural phenomenon, for example, Mitra, Surya, Savitr, Pushan and Adityas represented the solar god. Vishnu also had the characteristics of the solar deity. Later they were merged into one god Surya. As far the number of the gods is concerned, it is given thirty-three in many hymns, but in some hymns the number is largely increased many times. For example, in this hymn this number swells to 3339 while in the other it is 33.

92

Goddess Lakshmiji

"Three times a hundred Gods

and thrice a thousand, and

three times ten and nine have worshipped Agni."

–The Rigveda, III, 9,

"O ye eleven Gods whose home is heaven

O ye eleven who make earth your dwelling.

Ye who with might, eleven, live in a waters, accept

this sacrifice , Ye Gods with pleasure".

–The Yajurveda, VII, 19.

Gradually many gods became secondary importance, while others became more popular, and new ones came into existence, which were more anthromorphic than the previous ones. Thus on popular levels Hinduism is pantheistic, and henotheistic. The Hindus find the divinity expressed through many objects like a ray of the sun filtering through a prism. They may rever a lifegiving river, a god-man, a rishi, or any of the avatars of Vishnu as a manifesatation of his glory. All these manifestations represent the inner divinity in external form, and help in realization of the one Reality underlying the various expressions.

CHAPTER FIVE

Rites, Rituals and Observances

Religion is the pathway of realization and fulfilment, Religious practices, rituals, rites, customs and ceremonies are aids to the awakening and unfoldment of latent spirituality in man. They help on the path of spiritual growth and evolution, and gradually the grosser ones give place to higher and subtler ones. Ritual and rights have rightly been termed as the "kindergarten" of religious and spiritual education and learning. There are classes and grades as there are in other branches of knowledge and learning;lower grades followed by the higher and the higher by still higher ones till one realizes the self and attains final liberation or moksha. They are inevitable, and form the first steps leading to the heights of perfection and supreme fulfilment.

God is infinite knowledge, inflinite wisdom, love virtue, compassion and grace, but he cannot be comprehended in all his fulness at once, because of human limitations. We cannot understand God as he is, but stage by stage, only a little at a time. We cannot pour an ocean into a cup. Gradually the vessel is enlarged and expanded, and it capable to receive of him more and more. What happened to Arjuna when Lord Krishna showed himself in his cosmic Form at former's request. Arjuna was over-awed, bewildered,confused and terrified. He prayed Krishna to return his former form and shape. So it is step by step; higher practices must be preceded by the lower ones. Only the successful completion of lower grades can lead one to higher grades. Different religious practices mark the different phases of religious growth. They evolved with the evolution in human understanding of God. That is why there are rites, rituals, customs, celebrations, ceremonies, observances, idols and worship in Hinduism to suit the different tempraments, capacities and inclinations. The choice is vast and varied. One can choose according to one's capacity, aptitude and standard. But all practices aim at taking an aspirant towards truth from untruth, towards immortality from death, and towards light of discrimination and knowledge from the darkness of ignorance. Rites and rituals are in the beginning, when man does not know God so intimately. They form a sort of ladder, a bridge between him and the God. When he has attained God, his goal, there is no ladder, no bridge; gradually they drop off themselves. There are rungs in the ladder. These may be identified as worship, concentration, upasana, meditation, samadhi, etc. What is gross, manifest, extrovert and physical in the beginning gradually becomes mental, subtle, introvert and without adjuncts.

Hinduism begins with the familiar, easier and concrete things, for one cannot jump to the ultimate realization without passing through the various stages of progress. It makes allowance for difference in mental make up. Spiritual growth, abilities, skills and aptitudes, every act, each observance, however gross, routine and extrovert, contribute its mite in the gradual awakening of the spirit within. They are basically religious, psychological and intimately connected with man's evolution in moral and spiritual terms. For example, a Hindu Festival, Cathartic in nature, is characterized by fasting, purification, worship, austerity, vigil, vows, offering and worship of gods and acts of piety. Hindu festivals are a living example of finding joy through renunciation and self-denial. They are an exploration in the enjoyment of things without being bound or obsessed by them. There are many ways of fulfilment and spiritual evolution, spiritual powers can be awakened and developed even by external observances at least in the initial stages. As such, they form the best form of austerity and spirituality for the masses. Lord Krishna in the Gita has said, "I am the ritual, I am the sacrifice, the oblation, and the herb. I am the prayer and the butter, the fire and its offering". The all-inclusive Hindu view of immanence finds God and the universe identical and observes religious practices accordingly.

Rites, Rituals and celebrations are in the blood of man, and the Hindus are more so because mother Nature has been so rich, generous, beautiful and fantastic here as nowhere else. Man in essence is a celebrating man. With the advancement on the path of spirit and religion, his rituals and celebrations tend to become more sober, inward, mental and subtle and ultimately many of them fall of naturally. Puja and prayer give him a sense of paraticipation in oneness of life, a sense of cosmic fellowship. With prayer, meditation and such other practices dawns an awareness of being in the presence of God. They are repetitive and observed daily, nay many times in 24 hours. All things that occur again and again in a rhythmic cycle deserve our utmost care and reverence for they are the essence of existence. It is this sense that early aryans, and the Hindu masses even today are ritualistic and celebration oriented.

Rituals and ceremonies, as instruments, help in seeking God's grace and purification of the heart. The early Vedic religion was ritualistic, which aimed at attainment of heaven after death and happiness, peace and prosperity here in this life. There were many types of fire-sacrifices to suit every occasion, and they formed an essential part of daily and routine religious observances. Then the emphasis was on karma than on jnana or knowledge. The conception of final liberationor moksha was not known then. But gradually the influence of the Upanishads made the new ideal of moksha replace the old one of heaven, which meant not merely absence of suffering but presence of abundant happiness and pleasures in the abode of gods. Though rituals seve a limited purpose of attaining material well-being, physical health and happiness, but they cannot be dispensed with completely. One type of ritual is replaced by another. The Vedic yajana or sacrifire was replaced by puja or worship of the personal deities in the homes and temples, and it gave rise to elaborate and wonderful sculpture and temple architecture. The Purva Mimamsa later on revived the Vedic ritualism. Mimamsa, which literally means investigation or enquiry is based on the Brahmana portion of the Vedas. It dealt with various aspects of ritual, as a means of attaining some specific benefit or avoidance of some particular harm. In Inter times the findings of Jaimini's Purva Mimamsa were systematised and further elaborated in the kalpa Sutras, which served as "a kind of grammar of the Vedic Ceremonial."The Kalpa Sutras along with Grihya Sutras revived and continued the Vedic tradition of ritualisitc observances.

THE SACRIFICE

The Vedic man performed agnihotra daily, and periodically other sacrifices in order to propitiate gods to secure wealth, cattle, progeny and the like here and the heavenly existence hereafter. It was an activity through which he sought self-fulfilment and preservance of the universe. He knew that the universe owed its origin to the divine sacrifice. It was the chief means of two-way relationship of man with gods and the

Supreme Being. Religion is essentially a sacrifice, a puja and a prayer. It is a spiritual act and attitude which helps man transcend his boundaries of space and time. It is the pathway to immortality and the conquest of death.

Man becomes a god and immortal through sacrifice. Man's whole life is a sacrifice. The yajana or agnihotra is the outer reflection of the sacrifice that is taking place inside him. And it is the real sacrifice. In the 16 to 18 sections of the Chandogyopanishad the full span of life is beautifully contemplated as a sacrifice. "Man, in truth is himself a sacrifice. His first twenty four years correspond to the morning libation... His next forty four years correspond to the midday libation. His next fortyeight years correspond to the third libation....When a man feels hunger and thirst when he does not rejoice, then he is undergoing his initiation rite. When he eats and drinks and rejoices, then he is joining the upasada rituals. When he laughs and eats and has sexual intercourse, then he is taking part in chant and recitation. Asceticism, alms-giving, moral integrity, non-violence, truthfulness—these are the gifts of the priests.

Therefore, one says, "He will procreate, he has procreated", for this is his new birth. His death is the ablution after the ceremony. Ghora Angirasa, having told all this to Krishna, the son of Devaki added, "when man is free fram desire, in his last hour, he should take refuge in the three following :

You are impersishable

You are immovable

You are firm in the breath of life.

"This kind of ritualistic and sacrificial conception of life is found in a few other Upanishads also. In the Vedas, the sacrifice, as an act that forms an immediate bridge between the doer and his fulfilment, and as an act of creation, has been extolled every now and then :

"They who could not ascend the ship

of sacrifice, sink down in desolation,

trembling with alarm.

When Gods prepared the sacrifice with

Purusha as their offering,

97

Its oil was spring, the holy gift was autumn

summer was the wood.

They blamed as victim on the grass

Purusha born in earliest time

With him the deities and all Sadhyas

and Rishis sacrificed.

From that great general sacrifice

the dripping fat was gathered up.

He formed the creatures of the air,

and animals both wild and tame".

—The Rigveda, XLV 6 and XCI, 6-8.

"May life succeed through sacrifice.

May life-breath thrive by sacrifice.

May the eye thrive by sacrifice.

May the back thrive by sacrifice,

May sacrifice thrive by sacrifice".

–The Yajurveda, IX, 21.

In the Bhagvad Gita this sacrifice is in the form of renunciation of fruits of action. Every work becomes a sacrifice when performed without attachment and desire of fruits. The renunciation of the fruits that may result from an action is surrendered at the feet of the Lord. Detached and disinterested actions are desirable both for individual progress on the path of spirituality and the welfare of others. A desireless work becomes a sacrifice, a work of love and establishes a link between the doer and the God. Thus, each and every work is a ritual, a prayer if done out of love of the humanity and without selfish motives.

"Worship the gods with sacrifice,

and they will nourish you in their turn.

Thus nourishing one another

You shall reap the highest good.

Cherished by your sacrifice, the gods

shall grant you your desires.

A thief verily is he who enjoys their boons
without giving anything in return.
Longing for success on earth
they sacrifice to the gods,
for quickly success is born
from sacrifice in this world of man.
Of one unattached and liberated,
with mind absorbed in knowledge,
his actions become a sacrifice,
his entire actions melt away.
Brahman is all, the clarified butter,
the offerer and the fire.
Unto Brahman verily he goes
who contemplates on Brahman alone
in all his actions.

–The Bhagvad Gita, III, 11-12; IV, 23-24.

SAMSKARAS

The Hindu Samskaras or sacraments are the prescribed rites and rituals signifying the outward expression of the inner spiritual refinement growth and grace. They are part and parcel of popular Hinduism and are observed to guard against the evil influences and to obtain spiritual grace through the propitiation of various deities. They are social and cultural occasions when man can give expression to his joyous and felicitious feelings and even sad sentiments. As a very useful means, they provide the physical and spiritual refinement to the practitioner. Thus, they become the first steps leading to spiritual evolution and perfection. They represent the Hindu beliefs in regard to man's relation with gods and the Supreme Being. The scared fire, oblations, invocation, purification, prayer, worship, charity, blessings, festivity and sharing with the relatives and friends are the salient characteristics of a Hindu sacrament. Very comprehensive in nature, these ceremonies create a spiritual, social and cultural atmosphere, Very conducive to the all round development of an individual and the society as a whole. It is a series of observances and rituals which begins right with the conception and goes through the birth, initiation and marriage to the funeral rites. Their symbolical, psychological and practical significance is great and obvious. The Grihya Sutras contain all these sacraments and give necessary directions in regard to their observance.

CHILDHOOD SACRAMENTS

Man is the hero in the drama of life. He occupies the central place in the scheme of creation. God creates, but it is man who understands and apprciates it. The birth of a baby, emergece of a new spark of consciousness, is an important event. Every being is sacred and mysterious, but man is the most sacred, for he is the most intelligible being. To become a parent is to acquire the stature of a creator. It means continuity of life, of traditions and wisdom and religious practices. To be a father or a mother is an inborn sacred desire, a religious duty. It is a kind of paying of one's debt to the forfathers. That is why right from the conception onwards through various stages of birth and development of a baby, there are prayers, observances and religious practices. Procreation is a fulfilment which impart meaning to life. In the following hymn the sacredness of the act of procreation is proclaimed in glowing terms;

"Woman in truth is Fire, O Gautama, the phallus is the fuel, the hair the smoke the vulva the flame, penetration the coal, the pleasure the sparks. In this Fire the gods offer semen. From that offering arises a person. He lives as long as he lives. When he dies, they carry him to the fire. Here his fire becomes Fire, his fuel fuel, his smoke smoke, his flame flame, his coals coals, his sparks sparks. In this fire the gods offer a person. From that offering arises the person resplendent as Light.

–The Brihadaranyaka Upanishad, VI, 13-14.

Conception, birth, initiation, marriage, etc., are important treligious, social and cultural occasions, when certain rites and rituals are observed among the Hindus. In the Atharvaveda there are many charms and prayers in regard to successful conception of a male child, prevention of miscarriage, delivery and the safety of both the mother and baby:

"Unto the womb let a foetus come, a male one, as an arrow to a quiver; let a hero be born unto thee here, a ten month's son.

"And what excellent seeds the bulls generate; with them do thou acquire a son; become thou a productive milch-cow.

"As this great earth receives the embryo of existence, so let thine embryo be maintained, in order to birth after pregnancy.

—The Atharvaveda, III, 23 & VI, 17

During the period of confinement and till the eleventh day after the birth of a child, when purification ceremony is held, the mother remians defie and unclean. Then wife and husband together perform puja and samkalpa. They sip consecrated water and are purified. This water is also poured over the heads of the infant's parents. This ceremony, known as jataka-karma, removes all defilement and the mother and the house become clean and pure. The purohita who presides over the sacrament is given gifts of money, grains and sweets at the end of the ceremony.

Then follows, on the twelfth day, the Namkarana sacrament or name-giving ceremony. A name is an important and a sacred thing. A Hindu child is often names after a deity, a saint, a holy thing or an auspicious object. The qualities of a particular god or person are supposed to infuence the personality of the child so named. More often than not, a Hindu child is given more than one names. In the Grihya Sutras detailed directions are given about naming a child. It is emphasized that a name should be pleasing, auspicious, easily understood in its meaning and according to the family traditions. Namakarana samskar marks the ever increasing horizon of a child's activities. On this auspicious occasion all the near and dear relatives and frieds are invited, and after purification rites, the fire sacrifice is observed and oblations are effered to various gods including the nine planets. The father performs the samkalpa and then the child is given a name according to the day, hour, moment and the planet and constellation under which the child is born. The child is brought out in the open courtyard and made to look at the sun by the father. Prayers are offered to ensure the lon life (ayshyam) of the child. In the end presents are given to the purohita and the guests.

Annaprasana samskar is the occasion when the newborn child is given solid food for the first time after weaning. It underlines the physical need of the child. Food is a sacred thing. It is the source of all life and existence. Food is Brahman himself. Sacrifice is the food of gods. It bestows vitality and strength both physical and spiritual. On this day sacramental food is prepared amidst chanting of various hymns and given to the child. It is performed when the child has attained the age of six months. The gathering sit down to a sumptuous feast after the fire-sacrifice and feeding of the child. The woman folk sing songs and do arti of the child on this occasion.

Chudakarana (tonsure) or hair-cutting ceremony is another important sacrament. It is supposed to give long life and happiness to the child. The shaving of the head, the cutting of hair and pairing of nails remove impurities and bestows happiness, health and beauty. It is done either when the child is one year or three years old. The child is anointed with oil and then bathed in warm water by the married women. Then it is adorned with ornaments. The purohita performs puja and sacrifice and the child is made to sit on a piece of consecrated ground in a red square drawn by the priest. Then the barber shaves the boy's head, leaving the tuft of a hair on the top. This tuft of hair or shikha became a universal symbol of Hinduism. The women sing songs to the accompaniment of musical instruments and perform arti of the child. A prayer recited for the long life and health of the child on this occasion is as under :

"For just thee, O old age, let this boy grow, let not the other deaths, that are a hundred, harm him; as a forgetful mother in her lap a son, let Mitra protect him from distress that comes from a friend".

"Let Mitra or helpful Varuna, in concord make him one that dies of old age; so Agni he offerer, knowing the ways, bespeaks all the births of the gods".

"Thou art master of earthly cattle, that are born, or also that are to be born, let not breath leave this one, nor expiration, let not friends "slay this one, nor enemies".

"Let father heaven, let mother earth, in concord make the one that dies of old age; that thou mayest live in the lap of Aditi, guarded by breath and expiration, a hundred winters".

"This one, O Agni, do thou lead for life-time, for splendour, to dear seed, O Varuna, Mitra, king! like a mother, O Aditi, yield him refuge; O all ye gods, that he be reaching old age".

–The Atharvaveda, II 28.

UPANAYANA

Upanayana sacrament or investiture ceremony is a very important

102

event in the life of a Hindu boy. It follows the akshrarambha samskar, when a child is taught alphabets on some auspicious day when the sun is in the northern hemisphere. Alphabets, the source of writing and knowledge, are held sacred. This ceremony is held between fifth to seventh year of the child.

Upanayana, the most important sacrament, makes the next stage after akshrarambha. It initiates the recipient into and active life. On this occasion the boy is given the sacred triple cord to wear, and then his life as a Brahmchari begins. It marks the beginning of the first stage of life, when the boy acquires knowledge and learning under a competent guru and prepares himself for the second stage called Grihastha. The ceremony takes three days, and the teacher accepts the boy as his pupil to impart him a new birth and the pupil becomes a dvija, the twice-born. The first birth is physical and this one is spiritual, signifying the unfoldment of his mind and spirit.

Upanayana represents the ancient Hindu ideal of strick continence. During this period the aspirant studies scriptures and observes strict celibacy under his guru. This is the foundation of all other three ashramas, namely, Grihastha, Vanaprastha and Sanyasa. It aims at the student's all round development, the physical, the mental, the moral and the spiritual. It is a kind of transformation which helps in the realization of the self. Without it a Brahman boy is deprived of his privileged status and becomes an outcast.

After ablutions and purification rites, the sacrament beings on a auspicious day and hour fixed by the priest. After shaving the head, the boy is made to sit, on a dias facing east. The priest then offers him a new garment, symbolizing the beginning of a new life, raciting, "May the Goddess who spun, who wove, who measured and fashioned this garment, clothe you with long life! Put on this garment, endowed with life and strength". The teacher then ties a girdle of sacred darbha grass, symbolizing the spirit of austerity and penance, round the boy's body saying, "Here is this blessed girdle, friendly Goddess for our defence against evil words and the purification of our family, investing us with strength by inhalation and exhalation."Then the teacher offers his new pupil the deer skin and the staff reciting approprate verses from the scriptures. Then touching his pupil's heart with upturned palm he recites a prayer for the former's well being and happiness. The touching of the

103

heart symbolizes the mental and spiritual harmony and communion between the two. Thus, a new life begins for the boy and he becomes a upanita, one initiated into a life of perfect discipline.

After the completion of the studies in a Gurukula, the student returns to his home and takes a ritual bath. This marks the end of Brahmacharya and student life, and beginning of a new phase, when he ready to enter marriage and plunge into worldly life of Grihastha.

MARRIAGE

Vivaha or marriage is central to all domestic and social activities. A quarter of one's life is spent as a Grihastha in the attainment of the ideals of dharma, artha and kama. A wife is the main source of these ideals. Wife and husband are complementary to each other, and therefore, marriage is a sacrament which leads towards the unity and integration of the two persons of opposite sexes. Without marriage one is incomplete and unfulfilled. Marriage is the corner-stone of human relationships.

The marriage ceremony has many stages. The selection of the husband and wife is the first stage. Generally the couple belongs to the same caste, but now a marriage outside one's own cast can also be seen. In the selection of a bride and a bridegroom their family, age, physical features, education, social status, etc., are taken into consideration and horoscopes of would be life-partners are matched. Marriage preliminary consists in betrothal or engagement. During this stage the bride and bridegroom are examined, terms of marriage are settled and formal acceptance is given. The marriage proper consists of kanya-dana, marriage sacrifice and saptapadi. The bride is gifted to the bridegroom, and the latter then takes the bride's hand into his own, homa is performed and then they together walk round the sacrificial fire seven times. Mounting a stone symbolizing constancy and stability, looking at the sun as a witness, and at the Pole star, representing steadfastness, are other observances of the ceremony. Marriage is sacred and so indissoluble. Hindu marriage are generally arranged ones.

The marriage of the Sun-maiden Surya with Soma, the Moon described at length in the Rigveda is the model of Hindu marriage. These verses relate the marriage ceremony in general and especially the wedding of Surya, the daughter of the Sun. The latter parts of the hymn quoted below describe the rites of handing over of the bride to the bridegrooom as a gift, the samkalpa, clasping of the hands, taking of the bride home, and the symbolic circumambulation of the Agni, the universal witness:

"Soma was he who wooed the maid;
the groomsmen wire both Ashvins, when
the Sun-god Savitar bestowed his willing
Surya on her Lord!
Her spirit was the bridal car; the covering
thereof was heaven. Bright were both Steers
that drew it when Surya approached
her husband's home.
Let Pushan take thy hand and hence
conduct thee; may the two Ashvins on
their car transport thee. Go to the house
to be the household's mistress, and speak as
lady to thy gathered people.
I take thy hand in mine for happy
fortune that thou mayest reach old age
with me, thy husband.........
O Pushan, send her on as most auspicious
her who shall be the sharer of my pleasures,
Her who shall twine her loving arms
about me, and welcome all my love and
mine embraces.
O Bounteous Indra, make this bride blast
in her sons and fortunate.
Vouchsafe to her ten sons, and make
her husband the eleventh man.
So may the Universal Gods, so may the
Waters join our hearts.
may Matrisvan, Dhatar, and Deshtri
together bind us close.

—The Rigveda, X, 85

105

The samkalpa and kanyadana ceremony in regard to Sita's marriage with Rama is described by Valmiki in his famous epic poem Ramayana:

"Thereupon, leading forward Sita, who was adorned with all ornaments, and placing her before the fire, facing Raghava, the King Janaka said to the darling of Kaushalya's heart, "This Sita, my daughter, will be your partner in the Dharmic life. Receive her, may all good attend you!—take her by the hand. Devoted to her lord, she will be fortunate, always following you like a shadow. So saying, the king poured into Rama's hand water sanctified by mantras, as the gods and the rishis applauded saying, Excellent, excellent!"the celestial kettledrums sounded, and there was a great shower of flowers.

"Thus, Hindu marriage is a sacrament performed for social and individual fulfilment, continuity of race and customs. It is a religious institution, a sacrifice, a fusion of the parts into a whole. Man and woman represent the Purusha and Prakriti, the cosmic palarities. It is their fusion and integration which sets the wheel of creation in motion. Neither man nor woman is complete. As persons and individuals, they are merely halves.

FUNERAL RITES

Rites and rituals are natural to man. He cannot dispense with them. They are there in life, and after death too, performed for the departed by the survivors. The Hindus consecrate their lives through various samskars or sacraments. They believe in the reincarnation and the other world of the dead. The funeral rites are important for they pave the peaceful passage to the another world for the departed soul. Agni is the envoy to the gods and carries oblations. That is why the Hindus dispose their dead bodies by cremating. Cremation is a kind of sacrifice. The Hindus view the wholelife as a sacrifice, and cremation as the last sacrificial act in an individual's existence Thus, rites can be termed as man's manifestation of his deep religious desire to propitiate the gods.

It is customary to remove the dying person from the bed and place it on the earth. Ganga-water and tulsi (basil) leaves are put in the mouth of the dying, and a cow and other things are given to Brahmans in charity. The dead body is then placed on a bier and covered with a fine shroud, and carried to the cremation ground by the nearest relatives and

106

friends. The chief mourner, generally the eldest son of the deceased, leads the funeral procession. The ladies are not allowed to accompany the bier to the cremation ground. On the way to the cremation ground three halts are made. The dead body is then finally bathed and placed on the pyre. The chief mourner applies a burning torch to the pyre with the chanting of mantras, "Burn him not up, nor quite consume him agni; let not his body or his skin be scattered. O Jatavedas, when thou hast matured him, then send him on his way unto the fathers.......The sun receive thine eye the wind thy spirit; go as thy merit is, to eart or heaven. Go, if it be thy lot, unto the waters; go make thine home in plants with all thy members".(Rigveda, X, 16, 1 & 3)

After the body has been half consumed its head is split open with a bamboo pole by the chief mourner, and when the corpse has been consumed, to a great extent, the people walk round the pyre three times and go to the nearby pond, river or well for bathing to purify themselves. Then they go to the deceased's house and return from the gate to their respective homes. On the third day the ashes are collected for immersion into sacred waters and the kites fed. An earthen pitcher, filled with water, is tied to a peepal tree. The bones of the deceased are taken to the banks of the river Ganges and immersed there. The Kriya ceremony marks the end of the period of mourning, when all friends and relations collect and worship is offered to the deities. The priests are given gifts and the assembled people a feast. During the Kriya ceremony it is customary for the pundit or the purohit to console the mourners by dwelling upon the transistory nature of life and immortality of the soul. Texts from scriptures like the Gita, Garuda Purana, Kathopanishad, etc., are recited underlining the idea that death is not the end of life and existence. Death is inevitable and universal, it is a change and transformation, a door through which all the beings pass from birth to birth. Change and continuity or transformation and transmission are the two aspects of the same reality.

FESTIVALS AND FASTS

Hindu festivals and ritual observances are essentially religious, and a great source of spiritual and moral advancement. Like the deities of the Hindu pantheon, fasts and festivals are numerous and frequent. Sometimes they outnumber the days of the week. There are more festivals than there are days in a week. A Hindu festival consists of purification, prayers, worship, fasts, vows and other acts of piety. Being cathartic in nature, the Hindu festivals purify and strengthen the spirit within. They teach how to find joy through renunciation and self denial. They are an exploration in the enjoyment of sense-objects without being bound and obsessed by them.

As fast as a religious vow and observance is the best form of austerity for the masses and householders, which helps in developing the spiritual side of the aspirant. It has been a time-honoured religious practice since hoary past. A fast or a festival, accompanied by prayer, acts of charity, contemplation, etc., becomes a convenient means of spiritual growth, purification and self-control. They help people in striking a golden mean between penance and pleasure. The Hindus are famous for turning every possible opportunity into an observance of rituals, fasts, prayers, and terminating it with a feast and festivity. The Hindu festivals and fasts have their roots in very old ideals and traditions, and underline India's cultural affinity, emotional integration, common ethos, points of contact and bonds of unity in diversity. We give below a few representative festivals and religious observancs.

Buddha Purnima

Lord Buddha, the Enlightened and perfect One was born in Hindu Kshastriya caste of the Sakya clan in Lumbini Gardens in 563 B.C. He left home and renounced the world in search of the Reality at the age of 29, and attained enlightenment after 6 years, when he was 35 years old. He passed away and attained moskha at the age of 80 at Kushinagar, in the country of Mallas. Tathagata, the foremost of the spiritual luminaries was born, attained enlightenment and niravan on the very same day of Vaisakh Purnima, the Full Moon day (of April-May). It was again on the Full Moon day of July that he set in motion the wheel of Dharma and preached the first sermon to his five fellow ascetics, who had fled him when he gave up austerities seeing their futility. He taught them the Dharma in the Deep Park of Sarnath in Varanasi, now a great centre of Buddhist pilgrimage and learning.

The association of the same day, that is, Vaisakh Purnima, with three great events of Buddha's life has made it the most important festivals in the Buddhists world. Lord Buddha is regarded as the ninth incarnation of Vishnu, and so is held in great reverence by the Hindus. Buddha Purnima is celebrated all over the world with immense piety devotion and fervour. Special celebrations are held at places like Sarnath, Sanchi, Kushinagar and Bodh Gaya, where he had become the Al-enlightened One. At Sanchi some of his sacred remains are enshrined under a magnificent stupa. On this day of celebration, Buddha-images and portraits are taken out in a procession. Devotees of Buddha recite and read their holy scriptures, observe fast, worship Buddha at home and in temples and practice charity.

Budha's teachings, based on the Middle Path between the two extremes of sensuality and mortification, are more relevant today than they were even before. He taught the "Four Noble Truths of suffering and its cause, desire or selfishness, of the removal of that cause and the Eightfold Path which leads to the end of suffering". He preached that this world is full of sorrows because of attachment to sense-objects. Our sufferings are direct result of our desire and sense-attachments. This results into reincarnations and a ceaseless chain of rebirths, sufferings, sickness, old age and death. He declared that extinction of desires and attachment is essential for salvation, and the only way is to follow the Eight-fold path: Right Belief, Right Intention, Right Word, Right Conduct, Right Living, Right Efforts, Right Thinking and Right Meditation. He underlined the importance of striking a judicious balance between indulgence and asceticism, and it is what most of us badly need today. "Decay is inherent in all component things! Work out your own salvation with deligence", we Lord Buddha's last words to the Bhikkus, before he passed away and entered into Nirvana.

Ratha Yatra

Ratha Yatra or Car Festival is one of the most important Hindu festivals. It is held in Ashadha (June-July) throughout the country, and car-processions of Shri Jagannath (Lord of the Universe) are taken out through the main markets and streets along with those of Lord Valabhadra and Devi Subhadra. But the main and most imposing festival is held at Puri in Orissa. Puri is well known as Shri Kshetra or Jagannath Dham. It is one of the four most sacred Dhamas or Places of Pilgrimage. The other three most sacred Dhamas are at Badrinath in the Himalayas, Dwarka in Gujrat and Rameshwaram in Tamilnadu. Puri is also one of the ten famous Shakti Pithas. It is here that Sati's navel fell, when her corpse was dismembered by the Sudarshana Chakra of Lord Vishnu. Here she is worshipped as Godess Vimala and Shiva, her consort, as Lord Jagannath.

Thousands of devotees from all over the country and abroad collect at Puri to witness and participate in this most spectacular religious event. The twelfth century imposing Jagannath shrine, 60 kms. from Bhubaneshwar, is situated on Nilanchala mountain. For a devout Hindu, a pligrimage to Puri is a must and a life-long ambition. It is believed that a three days and nights sojourn at Puri will free a pilgrim from future cycle of births and deaths. Most of the year it is crowded with pilgrims, but on the occasion of Car Festival, Puri becomes an ocean of seething humanity. On this auspicious day Lord Jagannath is taken out in a grand procession, and on an enormous chariot, 45 feet high, 35 feet square, and supported on 16 wheels, 7 feet in diameter. The Car is shown being drawn by four wooden horses and driven by the idol of Maruti. On the three sides of the chariot are the three wooden statues of Rama, Surya and Vishnu. The car is painted yellow and golden and is called 'Nandi-Ghosha'. The chariot of Lord Valabhadra has 14 wheels and is 44 feet high. It is painted red and green and called 'Tala Dhawaja'. The wooden statue of Satyaki is shown driving the chariot. There are wooden idols of Nrisimha and Rudra Devas, who are his companions.

The third chariot of Devi Subhadra is 43 feet high and has 12 wheels. Painted in black and red, it is called 'Darpa-Dalan'. The Pandava prince Arjuna's idol is shown driving this chariot. Then, there are idols of Vana Durga, Tara Devi and Chandi Devi on the three sides of the car. One day before the commencement of the festival, the 3 km. route is swept clean by the devotees with the brooms, symbolising the melting away of pride, vanity and conceit. The yatra commemorates Krishna's journey to Mathura from Gokula at Kansa's invitation. The chariot procession goes along the broad avenue to Gundicha Temple. The Lord's Summer Garden Retreat, where they stay for seven days and then are brought back to the main shrine. At the termination of the festival the chariots are broken up and used to manufacture religious relics. Every year new chariots are made. The deities themselves are made of wood and renewed at certain intervals, when certain astronomical conditions are there. The wood selected for this purpose must also satisfy certain conditions.

110

The three huge idols of Jagannath, his brother Valbhadra and sister Subhadra are taken out of the Garbha-Griha of the main temple and installed on the three respective chariots parked across the courtyard. Then the massive chariots are pulled with the four rows of the strong ropes by the thousands of devotees along the 3 km. route to Gundicha Temple. First Valbhadra's chariot is pulled along, then that of Devi Subhadra, and next the car of Lord Jagannath. In the evening the chariots reach their destination and then after puja and other rites, they are taken into the Gundicha Shrine. On the tenth day, the deities are drawn back in their chariots to the main temple.

An outstanding characteristic of Jagnnath temple at Puri is that there is no cast distinction, and all are equal whether one happens to be a Brahman or a chandal or a shudra. The legend of the origin of Lord Jagannath is equally fantastic. Krishna was killed by a hunter named Jara in ignorance, and Krishna's body was left to rot under a tree, but some pious persons found his bones and placed them in a box. Later Vishnu directed a devout king Indradyumna in a dream to make an image of Jagannath and to place the bones of Krishna inside it. Vishwakarma, the architect of the gods was assigned the job of making the image. He agreed on the condition that he should be left undisturbed till the work was complete. A fortnight passed and the king grew impatient and entered the place, which made Vishwakarma angry, and he left the images unfinished. That is why the deities have neither hands nor feet. Indradyumna prayed to Brahma, who promised to make the image famous. Brahma gave the images eyes and souls and also acted as the high priest of consecration.

The king of Puri, the descendant of king Anantavarman Chodaganga, the original founder of the temple, alone has the right to carry the Lord's umbrella and other paraphernalia, and it is he who sweeps the path before the chariots. Over 6, 000 male adults are in the Lord's service, headed by the king. Some 20, 000 people are said in all to be dependent on the temple for their livelihood. The Jagannath temple is a kind of world itself. The festival is observed almost everywhere in the country where there is a temple dedicated to Jagannath.

Deepawali

India has the longest calendar of festivals and fasts in the world. All the Hindu festivals are rooted in myth, and myth is nothing else but a poetic form of history. Deepawali or the Festival of Lights is an important popular festival celebrated throughout the country in one form or the other. It falls on the last day of the dark half of Kartika (October-November). As a matter of fact it is a five-day festival, but the main celebrations are on Deepawali.

Deepawali is associated with several legends. One myth says that on this auspicious day Lakshmi, the goddess of wealth and good fortune, roams about and visits the houses of people. Therefore, people tidy up their homes, establishments and shops and decorate them lavishly to welcome the goddess. In the night she is worshipped with great devotion. It also commemorates the triumph of Lord Rama over Ravana, and Rama's Return to Ayodhya. It is also on this day that Krishna killed the demon Narkasura.

A few days before the festival, the houses, are white-washed and completely cleaned. The courtyards, the gates and the place of worship are decorated with bandarvars, flowers, intricate coloured paperwork and at night every nook and corner of the house, etc., is illuminated with earthen lamps, candles and fireworks are displayed. People get up early in the morning and have bath and then move about freely in an atmosphere of gaiety, mirth, rejoicing and festivity. Lots of sweets are prepared and exchanged.

On this occasion people ask for each other's forgiveness for the wrongs done knowingly or unknowingly, and mutual relations are re-established and strengthened. Thus, all enmity is forgiven and forgotten and people embrace one another. At night Lakshmi, along with Ganesha is worshipped, old accounts are closed and new ones are opened. People in throngs go about the bazars and streets during the night and appreciate the finest illumination. Special shops and bazars are also set up on this occasion, and there is a brisk buying of sweets, utensils, clothes, jewellery, toys, etc.

Deepawali also marks the advent of new season and the sowing of new crops. On this day begins the new Vikrama Era and new account books are opened. The famous king Vikramaditya, after whose name the era is, was crowned on this day. People greet each other and distribute sweets. In Bengal Kali is worshipped with great fervour on this day. The Jains celebrate Diwali as a day of final liberation and moksha of

112

Lord Mahavira. Similarly Swami Dayananda Saraswati, the founder of the Arya Samaj, attained salvation on this day. The great Swami Rama Tirtha also entered his final jal-samadhi on this tithi. At great Jaina shrines like that of Pavapuri in Bihar, and Girnar in Gujrat, special puja festivals are held, sacred scriptures read and recited and Lord Mahavira worshipped. Thus, this great festival of lights symbolises man's urge to move towards lights of truth from darkness of ignorance and unhappiness.

Ramanavami

Ramanavami or the birthday of Lord Rama is a major Hindu festival celebration all over the country by devout Hindus both Vaishnavas and Shaivas. Rama the seventh incarnation of Vishnu was born on the ninth day of the bright half of the chaitra (March-April) in Ayodhya, in the Treta Yuga, the Second Age. There is one God, desireless, formless, uncreated, True Being, Consciousness and Bliss, the supreme spirit, the all pervading, whose shadow is the world; who incarnates himself as Rama or Krishna and does many things, only for the love that he bears to his devotees; who in his mercy ever refrains from auger against those whom he loves and knows to be his own. Adi Kavi Balmiki in his celebrated Ramayana describes the advent of Rama thus:

"Then after the expiry of six seasons and on the completion of the twelfth month, on the ninth lunar day of the month of Chaitra under the star Punarvastu with the Sun, Mars, Saturn, Jupiter and Venus at Aries, Capricorn, Libra, Cancer and Pisces, and when the Moon with Jupiter entered Cancer of the Zodiac, Kaushalya gave birth to great and prosperous Rama with mighty arms, rosy eyes and scarlet lips, the joy of Dashratha and the adored of all people. He bore all auspicious marks on his fair body".

The Ramayana means the "Ways of Rama". It is held in the greatest possible reverence because it embodies the best of human ideals and a living sum of Indian character. As popular religious epic and great literary work nothing can inspire and enthuse us more than the Ramayana. A verse in the end of Ramacharita Manas reads:

"There is no age to compare the Age of Iron (Kaliyuga); in it, if a man has only faith and devotes himself to praising Ram's spotless virtues, he can escapes from the sea of birth and death witout further trouble.

Religion has been revealed with four feet; in the Iron Age one is of the most importance to whomsoever God has given let him practice almsgiving and prosper".

A fair idea of Ramayana's immense popularity can be had from the fact that there are about 350 versions of it in Hindi alone, and the name of Rama, as Rama! Rama! or 'Jai Ramji Ki!', is a common form of salutation among the masses.

The Ramanavami festival offers to us all an opportunity to imbibe at least some of the ideals and spirit enshrined in the ways of Rama. On this great day Lord Rama is prayed to and worshipped, and it is the surest means to be able to follow in his ideals. One who approaches his lotus feet with love, devotion and humility becomes noble, large hearted, pious, peaceful, master of senses and beloved of the wise. On this sacred day you should observe fast and practice charities. You should visit a temple or Rama early in the morning after bath, etc. You can also make a small shrine at home and install a picture of Sri Rama-Panchayatan in it and offer prayers and puja.

In Ayodhya, the birth place of Sri Rama, great celebrations are there; the temples are decorated, Ramayana is read and recited and a grand fair is held. At other places also icons of Rama, along with Sita and Hanuman is richly adorned and worshipped and other acts of devotion and piety are observed. Canting of the holy name of Rama, Sankiratnas and holding of lectures and discourses of Rama's life and teachings, for the benefit of the audience, are a common feature of the celebrations. People take vow to devote themselves more to thier spiritual and moral evolution on this occasion. Really, Ramnam is a great magic formula (mantra) and a wish-fulfiling tree (Kalpa Vriksha), and must be repeated, recited and mediated upon every now and then. Tulsidas has said that place the name of Rama on your tongue, like a jewelled lamp on the threshold of the door, and there will be light, as you will, both inside and out.

Ramanavami is also celebrated as the Vasanta Navratra and the celebration starts from the first lunar day of the bright fornight of Chaitra and lasts upto Ramanavami. On Ashtami Durga is worshipped. A fast is observed all the nine days and Durga-saptsati is read and an earthen pitcher filled with water is installed. Some fast only on the first and the last day of the period. Rama and Lakshmana had also performed worship

114

to mother Durga before killing Ravana. If you wish to achieve anything worthwhile, seek the Mother's grace and it is proper occasion. Rma and Devi, both symbolize the victory of good over the evil.

Ganesh Chaturthi

Ganesh or Vinayak Chaturthi is one of the most popular Hindu festivals, celebrated all over the land, as a birthday of Lord Ganesha, the elephant-headed God, on the fourth day of the bright half of Bhadra (August-September). The clay moulded figures of Lord Ganesha are worshipped during this festival and then immersed into the sea, river, pool or some other such water. Ganesha, is the God of wisdom, learning, prudence, success and power. His names are repeated in the beginning of every thing. As Vighnesha or the remover of the obstacles, he is propitiated at the start of very activity, whether it be a journey, marriage, initiation, house construction, the writing of a book or even that of a letter.

He is a great scribe and learned in the religious lore and scriptures. It was Ganesha, who at the dictation of the seer Vyasa, wrote the Mahabharata. He is also the Lord of Ganas, the Shiva's hosts. He bears a single tusk (ek-danta) and hold in his four hands a shell, a discus, a goad and a lotus and is always acompanied by his mount, the rat. Ganesha is a great lover of sweets and fruits. He is also the presiding deity of Muladhara Chakra (plexus) or the psychic centre in the human body where the Kundalini Shakti resides.

There are two very interesting myths about his birth and how he came to possess the head of an elephant. One myth relates that disliking Lord Shiva's surprise visits during her baths, Parvati formed her scurf into a man's figure and gave it life. Then, she placed Ganesha to guard her bath-house entrance. Shiva came and tried to enter but when he found his way barred he cut off his head. It greatly angered Parvati and so ultimately Shiva had to send someone to fetch another head for Ganesha. The first creature found by him was an elephant. Its head was brought and planted on Ganesha's shoulders.

Another version says that Parvati was blessed with a beautiful son. All the gods assembled to see and admire the son of Shiva-Parvati. They all gazed at the child except Shani, beacuase he was under a curse, which caused any being he looked at to be burnt to ashes. parvati insisted that Shani also looked at and admired her son. No sooner, did Shani do so than Ganehsa's head was burnt to ashes. Parvati cursed Shani for having killed his son, but Brahma intervened and comforting told her that if the first available head were planted on her son's shoulders he would be alive again. So Vishnu set forth on Garuda and the first creature he found was an elephant sleeping beside a river. He cut off its head and was fixed on Ganesha's trunk.

Similarly there is another intersting story which relates why he has only one tusk. On Ganesh Chaturthi the images of Ganesha are worshipped with sweet balls (laddoos or modakas), water, new raiments, incense flowers, scent, betel leaf and naivaidyas (food offerings). His mantra is repeated, he is meditated upon and worshipped and the naivaidya distributed as prasad. Brahmins are fed and given gifts. In Maharashtra this festival is observed with great religious fervour, pomp, gaiety and eclat and Ganesha idols are taken out in grand processions before immersion into the sea, and even otherwise Ganesha is a very popular deity and worshipped daily and invariably in the beginning of every auspicious work. The prayers offered to him are many, but below is given one which is very popular.

Victory to Ganesha, Victory to Ganesha, Victory to Ganesha, the Lord,

whose mother is Parvati, and father Mahadeva.

We offer Him the garlands of flowers and fruits.

We offer Him the sweetmeat of ladoos, and the saints their services.

Four-armed, and one-tusked, He is gracious.

Astride a mouse, His forehead is adorned with sindoor.

He bestows sight upon the blind and cure to the leaper.

To the barren He give sons and riches to the poor.

We offer Him sweets and ladoos, and the sages their services.

Our offerings of flowers, gardlands and fruits to Him.

Be gracious to the poor, O scion of Shambhu,

fulfil our heart-felt wishes.

We chant this laud.

Janmashtami

On the eighth day of the black half of Bhadra (August-September) was born Shri Krishna, the eighth Avtar or incarnation of Vishnu. Therefore, this day is well-known as Janmashtami or Krishna-Janmashtami. This auspicious day of birth of Krishna, the direct manifestation of Vishnu himself, is celebrated in all parts of India with eclat and great enthusiasm. In the Bhagvad Gita Krishna declares; "All this Universe has been created by me; all things exist in me", and Arjuna addresses him as "the supreme universal spirit, the supreme dwelling, the eternal person, divine prior to the Gods, unborn omnipresent". His life is celebrated in great detail in the Puranas like Harvamsha and Shrimad Bhagvatam. The circumstances in which he was born were quite peculiar and mysterious. He incarnated himself primarily to destroy evil and wickedness and to establish Dharma.

The demon King Kansa was a great and dreaded tyrant, but he loved his sister Devaki, and at her marriage with Vasudeva, he out of great affection, drove their marriage chariot. Then, all of a sudden an orcale told him that eighth born of Devaki shall be the cause of his doom and death. At this he would have killed her then and there, but for the intervention of Vasudeva and their promise to give him over each and every child born to them. They kept their promise, and Kansa killed all of their seven children one after the other to a great suffering and grief of the couple. They were kept in the prison under strict watch and in chains and locks.

So Krishna was born as their eighth son in the prison cell. But It so happened, with divine grace, that the guards fell asleep, their chains loosened and locks and the gates of the prison cell opened. Vasudeva took the child Krishna to Nanda's house in Gokula and exchanged him for a baby girl born there to Yashoda. When Kansa heard of the birth of girl child, he at once rushed to the prison cell, and lifted the female child high, catching it by the feet and was about to dash her against a rock, when it slipped from Kansa's grip and assuming the beautiful form of the Divine Mother Vanished Saying, "Wretch, thy destroyer is flourishing in Gokula". There was a great joy and rejoicing in Gokula at the birth of a son to king Nanda and queen Yashoda. Yashoda was quite unaware of the exchange that had taken place during the night.

117

The Janmashtami celebrations start right from the early moring with bath in sacred waters and prayers, etc., but the climaxes reaches in the midnight with the rising of the moon, which marks the divine birth. On this auspicious day, strict fast is kept and broken only after the birth of Krishna at midnight. The temples and homes are decorated, scenes depicting Krishna's birth and his childhood pranks, etc., are staged with models both living and inanimate. Child Krishna's image is put into a richly decorated swing and rocked with a tender care all the day by the devotees. At night after birth, a small image of toddling Krishna is bathed in Charnamrita, amidst chanting of hymns, blaring if the conches, ringing of the bells and joyous souting of "victory to Krishan".

In Braja Mandala, especially in Gokula and Mathura, this festival is celebrated with greatest possible religious fervour and enthusiasm and the special deliberations of the day are relayed on the air. People from distant places congregate to Mathura and Vrindavana on this day to participate in the festival. The piety and fast observed on this day ensure birth of many good sons, and salvation after death. Reading and recitation of the Bhagvatam and Geet Govindam are most recommended on this day.

Dussehra

Dussehra or Vijay Dashmi is a very popular Hindu festival, celebrated with eclat throughout the country. It is observed on the tenth day of the bright half of Ashvina (September-October).

It is a ten-day celebration, during which Ramlila which is based on the epic story of the Ramayana, is staged at various places in most of the cities and towns in northern India with elaborate rituals. During its performance, the Ramayana is constantly recited accompanied by music. It presents a fine blending of music, dance, mime and poetry before an enthusiastic and religious audience sharing every event of the story with the actors.

Struggle between the forces of good and evil, and the eventual victory of the former over the latter, is basic to the Ramayana theme. Rama symbolizes the best in humanity, and Ravana the evil forces. Dussehra in Sanskrit also means taking away the ten sins. The ten heads of Ravana, represents these ten sins and Rama destroys them. Ravana abducted

Sita with the help of another demon named Maricha. Ravana kept Sita in the Ashoka Grove and persisted in making Sita his wife, but Sita always thought of her husband Rama. Rama sent his messengers to Ravana and urged him to return Sita, but Sita always thought of her husband Rama. Rama sent his messengers to Ravana and urged him to return Sita, but the evil minded-Ravana refused to do so. Rama set off for Lanka with Sugriva, Hanuman, Angada, Jambvana and hundreds of other mighty monkeys. Ravana's younger brother Vibhishana, a noble soul and devotee of God, however, took refuge with Rama. Rama built a causeway in the sea to carry him and his forces across the water.

Rama, along with his young brother Lakshmana, killed all the demons and regained Sita. Finally, they returned to Ayodhya in the vimana Pushpaka.

On this occasion huge effigies stuffed with brilliant fireworks are raised at various open grounds and set fire to by Rama. The effigies belong to Ravana, his brother Kumbhakarana and son Meghnada. This marks the culmination and termination of the celebrations. Elaborate and gay processions depicting various scenes of the Ramayana in the form of tableaus, are taken out through bazars and main streets. Apart from all this, Ramlila is also performed as a dance-drama by professional troupes.

Dussehra festival held at Mysore, is one of India's most colourful phenomena. The spectacular procession taken out on this day is a veritable extravaganza. The colourful Dussehra fair and festival of Kulu is also very famous. Among the Ramlilas, the one staged at Varanasi under the patronage of the local Raja, desires mention. On this auspicious day Lord Rama is worshipped, prayed and meditated upon to obtain his blessings and favour. In old days the kings generally marched their forces on this day against their enemies, the day when Rama routed Ravana.

Navratra/Durga Puja

Navratras are observed twice a year, once in Chaitra, preceding Rama Navami, and then in Ashivin (September-October) preceding Dussehra. This nine-day Navratra commences with the new moon of Ashivin and terminates with Mahanavami, on the ninth lunar day of the bright half of the month. During these nine days, devotees keep strict fast and Durga

119

is worshipped. The style of observing Navratra in different parts of the country may be different, but its sole aim is to propitiate Mother Durga and to seek her blessings.

On Pratipada (first lunar day of bright half of Ashivn), an earthen pitcher filed with water and its mouth covered with green leaves and an earthen lid, is installed with invocation of Ganesha, the god of learning and wisdom, and then Durga is invoked and ritually worshipped with durva grass, flowers, leaves, lamps, incense, new grains, raiments, etc. Barley are also sprouted and grown in a pot on this occasion, and the same are worn in caps and on ears on the final day. Unmarried girls below the age of ten are also worshipped and given gifts during these nine days. The aspirants sleep on the ground and keep strict fast all these days. A clarified butter lamp is always kept burning before the installed pitcher during the celebration, and daily Durga-saptashti, Devi Bhagvat Purana and Devi Mahatmya section of the Markandeya Purana are read and recited.

In Bengal Durga Puja is celebrated with great excitement and festivity and huge puja pavilions, with tenarmed Durga are set up. Durga, the beautiful but fierce goddess rides her mount of the lion, killing the demon Mahishasura. In each of her ten hands she holds one of the god's special weapons; Vishnu's discus, Shiva's trident, Varuna's conch shell, Agni's flaming dart, Vayu's bow, Surya's quiver, Indra's thunderbolt, Kubera's club, a garland of snakes from shesha, and as a charger a lion from the Himalayas. A fierce battle raged between Durga and Mahishasura, but finally she killed him with a spear.

Durga Puja surpasses all the festivals in Bengal in its popularity and mass appeal. During the celebrations music, dance drama and poetry are performed before the enthralled audiences. The earthen images of goddess Durga are taken on the final day in triumphal processions from all corners of coverage on the river where they are ceremonially immersed. Dura Puja is more than a ritual as it invests the lives of every one, and produces a fevrish literary and artistic activity. Durga is supposed to visit her parents Himavan and mother Mena during these days only in the year. The final day marks the end of this brief visit, when she leaves for Mount Kailash, the abode of her lord and husband Shiva. Bengali ladies give an emotion-charged and affectionate send off to Durga, and the ceremony is characterized with daughter's departure to her husband's house.

Shivaratri

Shivaratri is both a festival and a vow to be observed. It means the "Night of Shiva" and is observed on Shiva Chaturdashi of Phalguna, that is, on the fourteenth day of the dark half of Phalguna (February-March). It is celebrated by the Hindus of all faiths and castes all over the country. The devotees spend the whole night in the four watches in meditation, japa, kirtan, and rading and recitation of Shiva Mahima Stotra and Shiva Tandava Stotra. The lingam symbol of Shiva is worshipped with gangajal, milk, curds, honey and clarified butter, Bael leaves, dhatura fruit, aak flowers, etc., are also offered to Lord Shiva in puja. Bael leaves are very sacred and dear to Shiva.

Devotees in hundreds and thousands collect at the Shiva shrines and spend the whole night practising devotion and piety. Special puja celebrationa are held at Varanasi, Tarkeshwar, Baidyanath, Walkeshwar, Rameshwaram and Ujjain. At Pashupatinath, in Nepal also, a grand celebration is held on this occasion. The devotees keep strict fast and do not take even drop of water. At Mahadeva, he is worshipped by various gods, including Brahma and Vishnu. He can easily be pleased to grant a desired boon. He is great and powerful god and one of the Hindu Trinity. He is Mahakala and destroys and desolves everything into nothingless, but he, as Shankara, also resorts and reproduces that which has been destroys and desolves everything into nothingless, but he, as Shankara, also resorts and reproduces that which has been destroyed and dissolved. His symbol of phallus symbolises this reproductive power. As a Mahayogi, the great ascetic, he combines in himself the highest perfection of assustere penance and abstract meditation. In this form he is a naked ascetic. Digambra, "clothed with the elements". He is also called Chandrashekhra, "moon crested"; Gangadhara, "bearer of Ganga"; Girisha, "mountain lord"; Kala, "time"; Maha-kala, "great time"; Pashupati, "Lord of the beasts"; Vishwanath, "Lord of the Universe"; etc.

A very interesting story is told by the devotees on this occasion to underline the significance of the vow observed on this day. Once, there was a hunter called Suswar. He lived near Varanasi. He earned his livelihood by killing and selling birds and beasts. One day he went on a hunting expedition, but was overtaken by darkness and could not return home. The forest was dense and full of terrible beasts of prey. For protection he climbed up a bael tree for the night. During the course of the night, he suffered the pangs of hunger and thirst on the one hand, on the other he was very much worried about his dear wife, children and old mother at home, who had been waiting anxiously for his return.

In his great anixiety, he wept and began to pluck the bael leaves and dropped them on the ground. Under the tree there was a Shiva-linga, and that night was Shivaratri. The hunter's worship, though performed unwillingly, highly pleased Shiva. Therefore, the hunter after his death, got a place in the blissful abode of Lord Siva, and after ages was reborn as a king, named Chitrabhanu. The king observed Shivaratri and did great penance on that day.

Holi

Holi is one of the four most popular festivals observed by all without any distinction of caste, creed, status or sex. It is observed on the full moon night of Phalguna. It marks the end of winter and the advent of spring season. It is a two-day festival. On the first night bonefire is lighted in the evening or night. Before being lit, it is worshipped and offered water and gains, then people go round it to perform pradikshna. Children make merry, womenfolk sing gay songs and adult also sing phag to the accompaniment of cymbals and drums. People enjoy fun and like to play practical jokes on one another.

The next day, people amuse themselves by splashing coloured water and throwing coloured powder on their friends, relatives, neighbours and even passersby. Noisy and colourful processions are taken out through the bazars and streets. In refined people it is characterized by songs, music, floral decoration and splashing of perfumed water. Sweets and visits are exchanged and cold drinks prepared at home, are seved liberally. People forget all enmity and embrace each other, with warmth and love and renew their friendship. New corn is baked and eaten on this day for the first time in the season.

There are several myths about the origin of the festival of Holi. According to one Puranic myth, there was a great demon Hiranyakasipu.

122

He conquered all the three worlds and made the gods to serve him, He forbade practice of peity and worship of God, and instead declared himself God. People were made to worship him at the point of sword. But his son Prahlad, a mere child, a noble and great soul, was a great devotee of Vishnu and always chanted his name and sang his glories. It infuriated his demon father and he ordered "Let this evilsoul child be killed".

To kill Prahlad serveral fatal means were adopted, but none succeeded. At last a big fire was lighted and Prahlad was made to sit in her aunt Holika's lap and she then she then jumped into the fire. Holika claimed immunity from fire, but by the grace of god, Prahlad came out of the fire alive and unscathed, but his aunt had died. The burning of Holi commemorates this event. It symbolizes the triumph of good over evil.

Kumbha-Parva

Kumbha means a pitcher or a water pot. In the beginning of the creation, the gods under the curse of Rishi Durvasa, were defeated and turned out of thier abode heaven by the Durvasa. They went to Vishnu and sought his help. He advised them to churn the ocean for Amrit or elixir. When the Amrit Kumbha (pitcher of nectar) appeared, there ensued a scramble between the gods and the demons, and some of its contents splashed out and fell at four places.

These four places are Hardwar or Haridwar. Prayaga (Allahabad), Ujjain and Nasik. Now, Kumbha Parva or Mela is held every 12 year in rotation at these places. It is called Purana Kumbha, and the one held every six years, after the full ones, is called the Ardha Kumbha (half Kumbha). At Hardwar it lasts for about a month and half in Phalguna-Chaitra, When the sun passes to Aries, and Jupiter, is in Aquarius. At Prayag, it is held in Megh (January-February), when Jupiter is in Aries, and the sun and the moon in Capricorn. At Ujjain planets are in Libra. It is held on the banks of the River Shipra. At Nasik it is held on the banks of the River Shipra. At Nasik it is held on the banks of Godwari, in Shravan (July-August), when these planets are in Cancer. These Kumbha melas terminate with the final bath on the new moon day.

Kumbha Fair is the most magnificent bathing festival ever held in the world. Millions of people, which include saints, sanyasis, rishi-munis, priests, naga sadhus, mahants and milling crowds from all parts of the country, participate in it. Sometimes, the rush of devotees is so unmanageable that in spite of great preparations for several months ahead, there is stampede, and the result is a mass tragedy. In the recent Kumbha Fair, held at Haridwar on March-April 1986, at least 100 pilgrims died and scores were injured. And it was not for the first time. The toll was much larger in 1975, when 500 persons died and it was the largest in 1760 when as many as 18, 000 pilgrims are said to have perished.

Because the Jupiter, the Sun and the Moon had helped in protecting the Amrit Kumbha from being snatched by the demons, the position of these three planets determine the principal bathing days. During Kumbha Fairs, there are continuous recitation and reading of scriptures, Epics and Puranas. There are religious discourses; food, clothes, money and other gifts are given liberally to the needy, saints, and sadhus, There are endless processions of mahantas in richly decorated swinging palanquins, of ashsmeared naga (naked) sadhus in endless file and others with their matted locks, either dangling lose around their heads or tied into a high knot above. Al holy dip during Kumbha Parva is highly meritorious, as it destroys all sins. The ancient Hindu scriptures wax eloquent in praise of these fairs. These reflect the true soul of india, the glory and greatness that India was, and still is, and the living faith enshrined in the hearts of millions and millions of Hindus.

Satyanarayana Vrata

This Vrata can be observed either on Sankranti, Ekadashi or Amavasya or Puranmasi. But in Northern India, It is generally observed on the full moon day (Puranmasi) of every month. Satyanarayana or Satydeva means the Lord of Truth, and it is another name of Vishnu. The merits obtained by onserving this Vrata are many. It destroys all sins and evils, and ensures peace of mind. bliss, prosperity, happy relations, health and truthfulness. In the Kaliyuga, worship of Lord Satyanarayana with devotion, is like the veritable wishfulfilling cow. There are many interesting legends in connection with the observance with the fast.

Once Davarishi Narada happened to visit the earth, the Mrityuloka.

He was very much distressed to find the people there in misery, ill health and poverty. He wanted to relieve the sufferings of the mankind, but could not find out any way. He went to Satyaloka and told all about it to Bhagwan Satyanarayana. Lord Narayana advised Narada to go on the earth again to tell the people to observe Satyanarayana fast on the day of Purnima or Ekadashi, Amavasya or Sankranti. Their evils, sins and suffering would vanish instantly and prosperity, happiness and bliss would be their sure lot, the Lord told Narada.

Narada returned to the earth and preached the message of Satyanarayana Vrata. People did accordingly. They observed strict fast, listened to the story of Satyanarayana, sang his praises and meditated on him, and had all their desires fulfilled.

On this auspicious day, the aspirants should get up early in the morning, after taking bath they should pray and worship Suryanarayana first of all, and thereafter invoke Satyanarayana. They should make a small pavilion with plaintain trunks, flowers, leaves, etc., and install therein an image or picture of Satyanarayana. Then, the Lord Should be ritually worshipped with camphor, fruits, lamps, incense water, naivedya, betel leaf, etc., and the story of the vrata shuld be heard from a Brahmin. The Brahmin should be given gifts of grain, fruits, sweets, money, etc., and then prasad shuld be distributed. And finally in the afternoon the fast should be broken.

There is another story which very beautifully underlines the spiritual significance of observing a vow on this day. There was a very poor Brahmin. He lived on alms and spent his days in misery. One day Lord Satynarayana took pity, and appeared before him in the guise of a pandit or learned Brahmin. The Lord ordained him to observe the Satyanarayana Vrata. The next day was Puranmasi. He prepared a simple prasad of baked flour and Sugar, and after worshipping Narayana with full devotion and faith, distributed the prasad, and partook of it and prospered.

On the next Puranmasi, he celebrated the fast on a grand sclae. A poor wood-cutter chanced to pass by his house. The poor wood-cutter heard the Satyanarayana katha, ate the prasad, and being inspired observed the vow himself along with his wife and children, with complete devotion and piety proper for the occasion. Consequently, he became very rich, enjoyed all the joys of life and after death attained the blissful abode of Lord Hari, the Satyaloka.

Satyanarayana Vrata is the easiest and most inexpensive way of self-purification and self-surrender at the lotus feet of Hari. One who observes it with full devotion and faith is sure to attain his heart's desire. Such a celebration creates healthy and pure vibrations and purges the heart of all dross and evils.

CHAPTER SIX

Yoga : The Science of Soul

Yoga marks the culmination of the spiritual growth through rites, rituals, observances, puja, upasana, contemplation and dhyana. It is the final stage when man realizes. 'Tat vamasi or Aham Brahman'. It is characterized by the end of attachment to things and sense-desires, leading to the identification of the knower with the Self or Atman. Rites and religious practices are a means of obtaining temporary gains and favours from gods, which man feels he cannot acquire otherwise, but yogic state is the state of complete fulfilment, bliss, peace, absolute knowledge and emancipation. Yoga represents the highest grade and class in spiritual learning and attainment. It is the final phase of religious and spiritual evolution. External practices are like formalities observed because one is still not intimate and united with the Reality. There are all kinds of rites and rituals when one wants gods to advance one's interests, not so high and sublime, but merely mundane and comparatively cheap.

The early Aryans exerted their best to propitiate various gods and goddesses through sacrifice and laudatory hymns and such other practices in order to gain their grace and avoid misfortunes and adversities. They wanted to lead a life full of longevity, health, pleasures, riches and laughter. They wished it to continue here after in the heaven in the company of Indra, Varuna, Mitra, Soma and other gods. That is why Vedic religion was more pantheistic and polytheistic and less monistic. Those were the formative days and the concept of yoga leading to final liberation and release through jnana was then perhaps not known. It was in the Upanishadic times that the ideal of heavenly joys and pleasures was replaced by moksha and final release. Upanishadic seers aimed not at life of joys here and a post-mortem existence of bliss in the paradise but sought after desireless jivanmukti here and perfect identification with Brahman and cessation of the cycle of birth and death

127

hereafter.

The urge to realise the Reality is there alike in the observances and Yoga, but later quickens the process of spiritual evolution by expanding the aspirant's consciousness. It is a direct method which does away with intermediaries and such other things which obscure the vision of God. Yoga is subtle, and therefore, for them who are introvert and jnani. Karmakanda and rituals form the path trodden by extroverts for the sake of material gains, sense-satisfaction and removal of adversities. Rituals are useful at lower levels for gaining favours and grace from God, for is bestows what he prayed for. A great part of the Vedas is in the form of Prayers, rituals and fire sacrifices meant for different occasions for obtaining specific fruits and desires. But in the Upanishads Karmakanda has been replaced by knowledge as a sure means of God-realization and moksha. it is in this sense that the Vedas represent the childhood of Hinduism and Upanishads the maturity and adulthod. Upanishads have the eye of archer Arjuna, and make their way directly to the goal without looking right or left. There is no distraction, no deviation and identification is perfect.

"This they consider as Yoga
The firm holding back of the senses.
Then one becomes undistracted.
Yoga, truly is the origin and the end.

–Kathopanishad, VI, II.

Distraction, lack of discipline and self-control, greed, glutony, anger, lust, levity, discontent, etc., are ayoga or mental distraction. Yoga is the sure panecea for all these and many more ills. Yoga generates in the heart of a yogi the virtues of renunciation, desirelessness, non-attachment, concentration, equanimity, harmlessness, purity, peace and love for all. These virtues are certainly far superior than the material gains and favours obtained from gods through sacrifice, rituals, rites and observances. The faculties of mind are weakened by attachment to things and desires while non-attachment desirelessness, freedom from the bondage of sense-objects and constant communion with Universal soul strengthen and help in the unfoldment of latent potentialities.

The origin of yoga can be traced back to Proto-Shiva of Indus Valley Civilization. There were excaved many terracotta statuettes of the three-faced god sitting in a yoga-posture and abosrbed in meditation of samadhi.

Lord Krishnji

He has his sight fixed on the tip of his nose. He is attended by a bull and surrounded by many other animals. This same god has been identified with Shiva of classical Hinduism. Thus, the cult of penances, austerities, concentration and yoga is originally pre-Vedic and non-Aryan. It was later on incorporated and assimilated into the classical Hinduism. "The Harappans knew the use of copper, but there is little indication of thier use of iron. In contrast, the Aryan invaders were essentially pastoral people. They used horses and chariots and had arrows of iron. Thus they were both physically and militarily better endowed than Harappans. Hence the Aryans conquered the Harappans and other pre-Aryan Natives of India. But from the view point of culture, religion and ascetic practices the Harappans and the pre-Aryan natives of India were superior. Therefore, in due course, the Aryan conquerors adopted a good deal of pre-existing Indians culture and religion. For this reason, it has been said that the Aryan God, Indra won the battles, but the non-Aryan God, Shiva Ultimately won the war".

The Upanishads have rightly been designated as Vedanta or culmination and consummation of the Vedas. The Upanishadic seers and truth-seekers delved deep into the mysteries of evolution and involution and analysed the thought process of yoga in great detail. The Vedic thinkers sought to attain heavely pleasures through sacrifice and other ritualistic practices. But the Upanishads declared the cessation of birth and death and the attainment of moksha as the summum bonum of human life. They found that post-mortem heavenly existence was a temporary phase which would terminate as soon as the merits earned through sacrifice were exhausted. They wanted a permanent solution to the problem of misery and human suffering, and they found the answer in the realization and identification of the individual soul with the Universal Soul through yoga. They tell, how through Yoga, one can attain the state of samadhi or transcendental trance through the awakening of bodily centres combined with constant meditation. The yoga-practice helps in developing certain extraordinary powers, but they are a sure hindrance in the attainment of final goal of Self-realization, and can even be a source of fall and degeneration. Yoga is not merely a system of thought, but a practical and elaborate technique based on the steady and persistent meditation as a means to God-realization.

Yoga is a very comprehensive term and may mean different things in different contexts. In the present context, yoga means yoking, joining together, communion, application, concentration, and mental abstraction. The term "Yoga, is derived from Sanskrit "yuj" which means what have been stated above. Yoga is the common foundation of all Hindu Philosophic systems and practices. It is a link, a union, which unites the indivdual soul with the Universal Soul by consuming all the past accumulated karmas and their fruits. Yoga is a process which accelerates this union of the soul and the Over-soul. One who practices Yoga is a yogi. Yogi-path is a path of total surrender, body, mind and soul to the wil of the Supreme Being. The thought process of yoga subdues the sense and desires, stills the mind, burns the samskaras, and thereby imparts an inexpressible equipoise. This balance and harmony help the spirit soar high above the reach of illusions and duality, in the realm of perfect bliss, rest, non-duality and fulfilment. It is a kind of religious and spiritual experience which is regarded as the most sublime ideal in Hinduism.

"When the five organs of perception are still,

together with the mind, when the reason does not function;

this they ever to be the highest state.

This they deem to be yoga—the steady

concentration of the senses. Man then becomes

pure attention, for yoga is both

origin and extinction".

–Kathopanishad, VI, 10-11.

Yoga stands for complete union of the spirit with the Brahman or Ishvara. As the pratice of self concentration, it is intimately connected with Buddhism. It is an all inclusive awareness a fathomless deep consciousness where all thoughts, samskaras, etc., get themselves dissolved and fused into a perfect harmony and equilibrium. Yoga as system of thought and techinque is an integral part of Hindu sadhana and God-realization. A yogi, having attained this state of mental equipoise, continues to live as usual, but then the karmas do not bind him with their fruits. He reaches a state which is beyond both good and evil deeds, pleasure and pain, in short, all duality.

"There a father becomes not a father; a mother not a mother.....he is not followed by good, he is not followed by evil, for then he has passed beyond all sorrows of the heart".

—Brihadaryanyakopanishad, IV, 3, 32.

"As water adheres not to the leaf of a lotus flower, so evil action adheres not to him who knows this Brahman".

—Chhandogyopanishad, IV, 14, 3.

If a man has the senses withdrawn as in sleep and a perfectly pure heart, he sees as if in a dream in the emptiness of the senses the pranava (Om), the leader whcse form is light, who is beyond sleep, old age, death, and sorrow. Then he himself becomes the one who is called pranava, the leader whose form is light, who is beyond sleep, old age, death and sorrow. Thus it is said:

When the yogi unites his breath with Om

Or is united with the all in the manifold ways,

It is called yoga.

This oneness of breath, mind and senses,

the renunciation of all existence—

this is termed yoga".

—Maitri Upanishad, VI, 25.

The great sage and grammarian Patanjali, who lived in the second century B.C., has defined yoga as "Chitravritti-nirodha". It means that yoga as a metaphysical system and technique is nothing else but the control and reorientation of mental modifications and fluctuations. The term "chitta" stands for mind, and "vritti" denotes the fluctuations of mind or its restlessness. The term "nirodha" signifies control or restraint of this restlessness. This constant mental restlessness can be controlled and eradicated by relentless regular yoga-sadhana. Thus, yoga symbolizes awakening of all the latent spiritual potentialities in a man or woman. It is meant for all men and women, without any distinction of caste, creed, sex or community. It paves the path—way going to essential unity and oneness of all living beings, and their identification with Brahman. Be seeing every living being as a partial expression of the Universal Soul, one realizes the oneness of life through yoga. Then, there dawns a deep sense of universal belonging, and one does not suffer from duality and division. It is a kind of depth awareness which enables the aspirant to acquire discrimination (viveka), non-attachment (vairagya), peace and equipoise.

SANKHYA AND YOGA

The man, who observe rituals and rites, are like children in the field of religion, but a few of them might be potential spiritual giants, who soon give up such religious observances and rites, and take to yoga as a direct means to accelerate their evolution, and reach the ultimate goal of salvation or moksha. The Sankhya and Yoga schools of philosophy are closely related. These two systems of metaphysics stress that salvation is to be attained not by rites and rituals, but through self-discipline, exertion, meditation and knowledge. Kapila was the earliest exponent of Sankhya and Patanjali of Yoga. Their aim and methods of approach are so akin that they are often known by a single name of "Sankhya Yoga". The only difference being this that Sankhya lays more stress on jnana or knowledge and is atheistic while yoga lays stress on meditation and has God or Ishvara over and above everything. The Ishvare of yoga is not the creator of the universe in the ordinary sense of the term. He is the perfect Purusha and an example to man to follow. Thus, God is one of the principles in Yoga for attaining salvation. It is total surrender and devotion to Ishvara combined with other disciplies which help the aspirant in achieving self-realization and release from bonds of human existence. Ishvara is not simply an ideal to be followed, but he is all mercy and compassion, and he helps the aspirants if they meditate on him and surrender at this feet. This God was symbolically represented in the sacred syllable Om (Aum) or pranava. It is a mystic moonsyllable, and an object of profound religious meditation. The highest spiritual powers are attributed not only to the whole word, but also to the sounds A, U, M, of which it is composed. Later on it began to represent the Hindu Triad of Brahma, Vishnu and Shankar and their union. Om has been the most sacred syllable, a mantra, representing Supreme Reality. The sadhakas chant and meditate upon it for self realization, fulfilment and attaining of moksha. It is regarded as the only syllable capable of symbolizing the ultimate reality and absolute Brahman.

The earliest work extant on Sankhya is the Karika of Ishvara Krishna, and that on Yoga is the Sutra of Patanjali, Sankhya system is based on the duality of Purusha and Prakriti or spirit and nature. Prakriti is all pervasive and complex and the first cause out of which this nuiverse is evolved. Prakriti is possessed of the three gunas or stsands, the satrva, rajas and tamas, and therefore, everything emanating from it possesses

Supreme Mother Goddess Durga

Goddess Durga — renowned slayer of demons, wife of Shiva,
personifying Shakti or divine energy.

these three gunas. The variety of the things is based on the different proportions of these gunas. Sankhya believes in plurality of spirits instead of One Atman. A Jivatma should gradually transcend these consitituent gunas, with the help of Viveka or discriminative knowledge. Sankhya is called so because it is based on discriminative knowledge, and also because it enumerates 25 Tattvas, 24 of which are evolved out of Prakriti the First cause or Primordieal Essence. The 25th being Purusha, which is neither Producer nor Production, but totally distinct from all other Tattvas. Sankhya aims at liberation of Jivatma from the fetters caused by the creation being produced by the contact of Purusha and Prakriti. Later on Prakriti came to be identified with the wives of the gods, especially with Shakti, the consort of Shiva. Purushas are innumerable. Through ignorance a Purusha begins to identify himself with the body, the evolute of Prakriti. It is viveka which makes a soul realize its true nature of being pure, uninvolved, unattached and devoid of any acitivity. Age, death, suffering, pleasure, pain etc. belong to the body. Therefore, man can work out his own liberation by possessing the jnana of the real nature of Purusha and Prakriti. Sankhya helds that there are souls but no Oversoul or Ishvara. It denies the existence of God and holds that he is not required at all for the salvation of a soul. There is no necessity of Ishvara for the universe is self-existent and things evolve from Prakriti without his intervention. Thus, Sankhya, Buddhism and Jainism have much in common. They all believe that bondage is because of avidya or nescience. Bondage entails birth and rebirth, death, suffering and pain, however, these can be overcome and salvation achieved by man's own exertion through discriminative knowledge or viveka.

THE FOUR PATHS

Archaeolovically the story of yoga can be traced back to the Indus Valley Civilization, but it is Vedanta or the Upanishads which laid the firm foundations of this science of soul and life. The identification and unity of the soul with of versoul or Brahman and final release is central to all the yoga philosophies and systems. After the Vedanta, the Bhagavada Gita is the best known of all the treatises on yoga. Hinduism gives due consideration to the difference in mental make up, aptitude, etc., found in men. Therefore, there are four main paths of yoga to choose from to one's temperament, inclination and approach. All these paths ultimately converge on that one and same centre. The goal is one, paths may be different. The following are the four main Yoga-Paths:

1. Krma Yoga
2. Bhakti Yoga
3. Jnana Yoga
4. Raja Yoga

1. Karma Yoga

Karma means any action done voluntarily. A karma is a cause resulting in a definite effect, bad or good according to the action performed. The doer has to enjoy or suffer the results of his good or bad karma. He cannot escape it. Man enjoys the fruits of his past karmas and sows new seeds of action to be reaped in the next birth. Nobody can escape the karmas and their fruits. This creates an unending cycle of births and deaths. Fruits of our actions are to be consumed and exhausted. Thus, our karmas cause Samskaras and ceaseless bondage and suffering. Samskaras are impressions on the mind of acts done in a former state of existence. Work is natural to man. Complete cessation of work at any stage of life is impossible. As long as there is life and body there are actions. In the Gita Lord Krishna declares, "None can ever remian really actionless even for moment, for everyone is helplessly driven to action by the Gunas, born of Prakriti". Work is essential and obligatory, none can dispense with actions:

> "Engage yourself in obligatory work
> for action is superior to inaction
> and if inactive, even the mere
> maintenance of your body would not be possible".

—The Gita, III, 8.

Actions are essential in this sense also that they are imitated and followed by others. Therefore, the people go by the example a great man sets up. Krishna is an incarnation of God. He has nothing to gain by performing acts. He has no desires to satisfy, no wish to fulfil, but even then he works for the good of the world:

"There is nothing in the three worlds,

134

that has not been done by Me,

nor anything that might be attained;

still I engage in action.
If ever I did not work relentless,
O Partha, men would in every respect
follow my path.
These worlds would perish if I
did not do action; i should be
the cause of confusion of species
and should destroy these beings".

–The Gita, III, 22-24.

In such a state of bewilderment, where actions and their bondage are inevitale, Karma Yoga offers the only solution to the problem. In it lies the greatest hope for mankind, engaged in various worldly actions. It teaches how to attain worklessness in work, how to perform action without their fruits or bondage. Nishkama Karma is the only penance of this ubiquitous disease of bondage. In the Bhagvad Gita, Shri Krishna Urges Arjuna to perform his duty as a warrior prince without any desire and egoism. A work done, not in the capacity of a doer or an agent, but as an instrument in the hadns of God, without attachment, without desires and ego, without any consideration of success or failure, is the real nishkama and nrivatti karma. A work, done in this spirit, neutralize its bindling effects. It is the renunciation of the fruits that is desirable, and not the non-action or renunciation of karma. Inaction in action is the ideal state. Shri Krishna asks Arjuna to perform his dharma as a solider absorbed in yoga.

"Seek to perform your duty; but lay not
claim to this fruits. Be you not the producer
of the fruits of karma; neither
shall you lean towards inaction.
Perform action, O Dhananjaya, being fixed
in yoga, renouncing attachments,
and even-minded in success and failure;
equilibrium is verily yoga.

The wise, imbued with eveness of mind,
renouncing the fruits of their actions,
freed from the fetters of birth
verily go to the stainless state".

—The Gita, II, 48-49, 51.

Arjuna is urged to fight without identifying himself with it. Yoga is equipoise, and it is obtained when man acts with his mind established in the se'f. It is really an illusion to consider oneself the doer of actions because, in fact, they are performed by the trigunatmika Prakriti. A karma yogi transcends three gunas by keeping himself aloof and unttached. A work done selflessly, without attachment to fruits thereof, becomes Nrivatti Karma. The way to liberation lies in work without being identified with it. The right action is one that does not bound, and hence it is detached and desireless:

"But even these actions should be
performed giving up attachment
and the fruits, O Partha;
such is My certain and best belief.

—The Gita, XVIII, 6

Non-action and lethargy is verily Tamasika. It is never proper to give up one's obligatory duty. The work done in a spirit of renunciation of its fruits is truly Sattvika, and so desirable:

"Whatever obligatory work is done,
O Arjuna, because it ought to be done,
abandoning attachment and also fruit,
That abandonment is deemed to be Sattvika.
The relinquisher imbued with Sattva
and a steady understading and
with his doubts dispelled, hates not
a disagreeable work nor is attached
to an agreeable one.

—The Gita, XVIII, 8-10.

Renunciation and performance of action both liberate man. But the former is too difficult a path to tread, while the other is relatively easier and best suited to the majority of the people. Giving up work externally is not the aim, for them sense cravings continue rsulting in fresh bondage. Thinking is also an act. Therefore, what is desirable is work willingly performed without any obsession and attachment. A karma-yogi is never disturbed by the possible success of failure or any kind of duality in regard to his work, because he holds himself as a mere willing instrument. In nishkama karma, knowledge and work are perfectly harmonized, and hence his equipoise and calmness remains unaffected and unchanged.

"He who is free from the notion of egoism
and whose understanding is not tainted
though he kills the people,
he kills not, nor is he bound".

–The Gita, XVIII, 17.

Every action is inaction where done while established in yoga, and such an action loses its binding effects. A yogi offers the fruits of his action to the Lord. he knows well that he has a right to perform an action, and not to the fruits of it. Karma Yoga is the pathway leading to jnana and moksha. With the cessation of desires for fruits, actions themselves become inaction and lose thier potency to bind. It is the path of purity, knowledge, peace, equipoise and true renunciation. When a work is done as an offering to God, it gives supreme purity and bliss, but only the best is offered to God. Hence, only the Sattvika actions, done dispassionately, without any touch of ego, and with perfect mental equipoise, should be offered to the Lord. A work done in this spirit evolves into a nishkama karma and takes the instrument of it toward liberation. An obligation discharged without involvement, attachment and hatred, without any hankering after its fruit, is really Sattvika.

"An action which is ordained, which is free
from attachment, which is done without love
or hatred by one not desirous of the fruit
that action is declared Sattvika".

–The Gita, XVIII, 23.

But a work becomes Rajasika when done with desires or with egoism, or unwillingly with much efforts. The same work becomes Tamasika if

137

done from delusion and with out consideration of the consequences.

As we have already seen that all men are not alike in their mental make up, aptitude and standard of mental achievement, and so they require different methods and techniques to evolve. The path of karma yoga suits them best who are active. They, by following their duties and dharma selflessly, dispassionately, and devoutly, without any thought of success or failure, can sublimate and purify their soul to the level of perfection and thereby obtain salvation

2. Bhakti Yoga

All the Yoga-paths overlap one another and lead to the same and one Reality. Bhakti is the path of devotion and total surrender to personal God. Here the realization and final release is through grace of God. Relatively this path is easier, and so its mass appeal is obvious. Brahman in his personal aspect is immanent, has attributes, adjuncts and a form. This aspect of God suits the great majority of the Hindus in comparison to the impersonal, formless and figurative absolute aspect, which appeals only to the exceptionally, well cultivated few. In personal aspect all human virtues are attributed to God, and yet he is free from all human limitations. Human mind and knowledge are finite and they cannot comprehend Brahman in all its infinity. Therefore, it is natural that when man tries to comprehend God, he superimposes all the human qualities on him, and he becomes personal, relative, possessed of a form and adjuncts, active, creator, preserver and destroyer. For a devotee he is the sole refuge, the father, mother, guru, brother, friend, solace, support and ultimate goal. He incarnates himself in human form at critical times when dharma is at its lowest ebb. He descends on the earth to establish dharma and righteousness, to preserve the noble and righteous and to destroy the wicked and demonic.

"Whenever there is decay
of dharma and rise of adharma,
then I embody Myself, O Bharata.
For the protection of the good,
for the destruction of the wicked and
for the establishment of dharma

138

I am born age after age".

−The Bhagavad Gita, IV, 7-8.

Bhakti cult, as such, is of later origin, but it has been a tremendous force and religious movement since its inception. The ritualistic propitiation of gods in the Vedic times was later on replaced by the concept of God-relization and attainment of moksha through intense devotion and Bhakti. Today its hold on the Hindu masses is phenomenal, and innumerable temples dedicated to various gods and goddesses and the worship offered to them there and in the house, is a sure sign which indicates what a great religious movement and living force Bhakti has been in India.

Bhakti Movement originated in Tamil country in South about first century B.C. and since then its sweep and hold on the Hindus all over the country, has been firm and constant. It was brought to North India by Ramanuja in the eleventh century. Right from the earliest the great Vaishnava Tamil saints (3rd to 8th century A.D.), known as Alavars and Nayanars, to the present day, India has produced great Bhaktas including Ramanuja, Madhva, Ramananda, Kabir, Nanak, Ravidas, Dadu, Tukaram, Purandar Das, Chaitanya Mahaprabhu, Surdas, Tulsidas, Meera, Samarth Ramdas, Swami Ram Krishna and scores others. They were not only great devotees but also great philisophers, hymnodists and authors, and have produced rich and immortal Bhakti literature. They were also great reformers and servants of the society. The entire Hindu world owes an incalculable debt to these great singers, saints and philosophers.

In the words of Basham, "Ramanuja's God was a personal being, who was full of love for his creation. He could even override the power of karma to draw repentant sinners to him. Unlike the impersonal World Soul of Sankara, which made the illusory universe in a sort of sport (lila), Ramanuja's God needed man as man needed God. By forcing the sense Ramanuja interpreted the words of Lord Krishna, 'the wise man I deem my very self', to imply that just as man could not live without God, so God could not live without man. The individual soul, made by God out of his own essence, returned to its maker and lived forever in full communion with him, but was always distinct. It shared the divine nature of omniscience and bliss, and evil could not touch it, but it was always conscious of itself as am I, for it was eternal by virtue of its being a part of godhead, and if it lost self-consciousness it would cease to exist. It was one with God but yet separate, and for this reason the system Ramanuja was called visistadvaita, or 'qualified monism'. Ramanuja was not as brilliant a metaphysician as Sankara, but Indian religion perhaps owes even more to him than to his predecessor. In the centuries immediately following his death his ideas spread all over India,and were the starting-point of most of the devotional sects of later times".

In the Bhagvad Gita and the Narada Bhakti Sutras, the subject of Devotion has been delineated in great detail in verses and terse aphorisms. In the Gita Lord Krishna categorically states; "Neither by the study of the Vedas, nor by austerit nor by gifts, nor by sacrifice can I be seen in this form as you have seen Me. But by unswerving devotion can I, of this form, be known and seen in reality and also entered into, O scorcher of foes. He who does work for Me, who looks on Me as the Supreme, who is devoted to Me, who is free from attachment, who is witout hatred for any being, he comes to me, O Pandava" (XI, 53-54). Intense love, devotion,total surrender, incessant remembrance, renunciation, purity, self-control, self-obnegation are the hall marks of true Bhakti.

Devotion is of two kinds : Para and Apara. Former is superior to the latter in the sense that it is totally desireless, there is no bargaining, and the devotee sees. Him alone, hears Him alone, speaks of Him alone and thinks of Him alone. It is devotion pure and unalloyed, devoid of any sense of separateness from the Godhead. In this regard Gopi's love for Shri Krishna is cited as the best form of dovotion and Bhakti. The followig psalm from saint Tukaram marvellously brings out the intense love, longing and pnags of separation suffered by a devotee's heart :

"As on the bank the poor flish lies

    And gasps and writhes in pain,
Or as a man with anxious eyes
    Seeks hidden gold in vain,
So is my heart distressed and cries
    To come to thee again.
Thou knowest, Lord, the agony
    Of the lost infant's wail,
Yearning his mother's face to see

(How oft I tell this tale!)
O at thy feet the mystery
    Of the dark world unveill
The fire of this harassing thought
    Upon my bosom preys.
Why is it I am thus forgot?
    (O, who can know thy ways?)
Nay, Lord, thou seest my hapless lot;
    Have mercy, Tuka says".

In Bhakti, it is love, pure, intense, all-inclusive and ever constant that forms the only measuring-rod :

"Thy nature is beyond the grasp
    Of huan speech or thought.
So love I've made the measure-rod,
    By which I can be taught.
Thus with the measure-rod of love
    I meet the infinite.
In sooth, to measure him there is
    None other means so fit.
Not Yoga's power, nor sacrifice,
    Nor fierce austerity,
Nor yet the strength of thought profound
    Hath ever found out thee.
And so, says Tuka, graciously,
    Oh Kesav, take, we pray
Love's service that with simple hearts
    Before thy feet we lay".

The paths of karma, bhakti and jnana not only overlap and gainfull intersect one another, but it is also desirable that they are judiciously combined to reach the goal of salvation. The Bhagvad Gita underlines and teaches "a life of activism grounded upon knowledge and centralized around the adoration of the Lord". Ultimately the three streams coalesce and form a kind of confluence where the ecstatic union with Ishvara is realized by the aspirant. There cannot be any watertight compartments and division of Yoga into various paths is owing to the difference in the general mental make up and aptitude of the people. Even in Bhakti cult itself the difference in individual inclinations and tastes is given due consideration. Therefore, it is enjoined that one should devout oneself to one's favourite deity, Vishnu, Shiva, Rama, Krishna, Ganesha, Mother Goddess or any other manifestation of God, but without any hatred and discrimination against any other expression of divinity. Each cult has contributed in the growth and development of another cult. Great exertion, attention, devotion and intense eagerness are common to Bhakti, Jnana and Karma alike. They differ initially to suit the different mental make ups and temperaments, but in the ultimate consummation they are akin and alike.

3. Jnana Yoga

Man's intense desire to seek release from bondage born of ignorance, and search for the truth, leads him to Yoga. But one man differs from the other in mental make up spiritual standard and aptitude. Therefore, what path and technique suit one, may not suit another. That is why there are different paths going to the same goal. An intelligent man possessed of contemplative bent of mind, would naturally take to jnana Yoga, the path of knowledge and discrimination, though it is said to be the most difficult one. But then, man enjoys best achieving that which is most difficult to attain.

Man is the most intelligent and national being. Retionality at its best lies in the discrimination of the real and true from false, and ephemeral. The Jnana Yoga is based on the rock-foundation of unreality of everything except Atman or Brahman. The world of names, forms and colours is a mere illusion. Since all appearances are deceptive, they are unreal and not permanent. Only Atman is the only Reality. Thus, unreality of things, and reality and eternity of Atman is the article of faith with the seeker of truth, and yogi. A jnan yogi exercises his faculties of reason, and treads the path of wisdom. And it requires tremendous moral and intellectual strength on the part of such an aspirant. He enquires into the nature of everything, including himself, through discrimination and determination. Self-realization and communion with Absolut, demand persistent efforts, relentless search and sadhana.

He knows, believes and realizes the essential undelying unity of all the creation. He knows that he is Thta, he is Brahman, and all others also are Atman. All are That; the Atman, the experiencer of all beings, is verily That. He realizes that Atman is all-pervasive, eternal, changeless, Sat-Chitta-Anand; Existence-knowledge-Bliss absolute. This he realizes by intense meditation and sadhna, by raising himself to the level of super-consciousness, where there is no duality. Then he becomes jivanamukta and attains liberation. Thus, the state of release and moksha is not a post-mortem stage but a reality here and now, in this very life. The belief terminates in realization. This marks the end of the quest and sadhana; the centre of gravity is now totally transferred to the self

It is the most difficult of the four paths, but in the same proportion does its desirability increase. Underlying this fact, the great saint poet and Bhakta Tulsidas says in his famous work, the Ramayana:

"In this manner is kindled the splendid lamp, ablaze with highest wisdom, in which the gnat-like swarms of vanity and other vices are consumed as soon as they approach it.

"I am that–'this unalterable persuasion (of the identifucation of the self with God) is its pre-eminently brilliant flame, and the happiness that results from this knowledge of self is the light it diffuses, by which it destroys the erroneous distinctions which are born of the world. Illusion and all the other forms of darkness that attend upon tyrant ignorance are utterly dispersed. Thus Reason having procured a light sits in the chamber of the heart and tries to loosen the knot; should he succeed in untying it, the soul obtains its object. But when Maya, O Garur, sees him loosening the knot, she creates many difficulties and sends forth, Brother, innumerable elves and fairies to tempt the Reason to avarice. In some way or other, by force or by fraud, they get near and try to put out the lamp by a side puff. If Reason is altogether wise, he perceives their hostile intent and will not look at them. Should he escape free from this danger, the gods then proceed to attack him. The faculties of sense are so many portals, at each of which a god sits on guard. When they see any sensual air stirring, they at once throw the doors wide open. If the blast penetrates the chamber of the soul, it forthwith extinguishes the lamp of knowledge. When its light is put out, there is no untying the knot, for Intelligence is undone by this blast of sensuality. Neither the senses nor the gods approve of wisdom; they are always inclined to sensual enjoyment. When intelligence has been thus fooled by the breath of sensuality, who can light the lamp again as before?

"Then, Garur, the soul is again subjected to all the manifold miseries of transmigration. Hari's delusive power is trackless ocean that none can traverse. Wisdom is diffucult to describe, difficult to understand, difficult to master, and if by any lucky chance a right judgement be formed, still many impediments block the way.

"The way of knowledge is like the edge of a scimitar; for those who fall on it, Garur, there is no escape. If any traverse the path in spite of its difficulty, they attain to the supreme sphere of beatitude. But this exalted felicity is immensely hard of attainment, as is declared by the saints, the Puranas, the Vedas and all the scriptures".

It is easier to concetrate on personal God, who is with attributes and adjuncts, but in Jnana Marga the aspirant meditates upon formless, figurative absolute Brahman. It is a path of negation, where the sadhaka negates every attribute, form and name in the Upanishadic spirit of "neti, neti"(Not this, not this), and therby arrives at the Reality, and true identity with it. The aspirant refuses to accept any other thing, but the eternal Reality. Jnana is knowledge, practice and realization, all rolled into one. It purifies and consumes all the sins and samskaras. Lord Krishna urges Arjuna in the Gita to seek this knowledge and enlightenment by enquiry and service:

"Knowing this, you will not fall into this confusion;

by this you will see the whole of the creation

in yourself and Me.

Even if yoy be most sinful of all sinners,

yet shall you cross over all sin

by the raft of knowledge.

As this blazing fire reduces fuel to ashes,

O Arjuna, so does the fire of knowledge

reduce allkarmas to ashes.

Verily there is no purifier in this world

like knowledge. He that is perfected

in yoga realizes it in his own heart

in due time".

–The Gita, IV, 35-38

Ponting the path and technique of jnana Krishna says:

"With work absolved in yoga,
and doubts rent as under by knowledge,

O Dhanajaya, action do not bind
him who is poised in the Self.
Therefore, severing with the sword of knowledge
this ignorance-born doubt about the self,
dwelling in your heart, be established
in yoga. Stand up, O Bharat!"

–The Gita, IV, 41-42

"With his intellect set in firmness
let him at ain quietude little by little;
with the mind fixed on the self.
Let him not think of anything.
By whatever cause the wavering
and unsteady mind wanders away,
let him curb it from that,
and subjugate it solely to the Self".

–The Gita, VI, 25-26.

Thus, yoga entails constant, deep and prolonged sessions of meditation till the desired depth experience and the insight leading to self-relization down. Control of senses and mind. coupled with Vairagya (reunciation) and sradha, is basic to jnana yoga. When the senses are not subjugated, the mind is led astray by the senses, and then man develops attachment to them; from it comes desire, and from desire arise delusion, confusion and ruination leading to damnation. A fickle-minded man can never acquire knowledge, and so the question of contemplation and meditation does not arise for him. 'Subjugation' here means control and sublimation, and never suppression. Again the Gita shows the path:

"He who is unattached everywhere,
who is not delighted at receiving good
nor dejected at coming by evil,
is poised in wisdom.
Sense objects drop out
for the abstinent man, though

145

not the longing for them. His longing

also ceases when he intuits the Supreme.

The excited senses, O son of Kunti,

impetuously carry away the mind

of even a wise man,

striving for perfection".

–The Gita, II, 59-60

4. Raja Yoga

Yoga is a spiritual discipline, which enables a jivatma to identify himself with, or be united to God or Brahman. It is a discriminative knowledge which helps one in attaining salvation by removing the bondage caused by ignorance or avidya. It is avidya which causes the confusion of taking non-self as Self and non-permanent as permanent. The Yoga Sutras of Patanjali, consisting of 185 sutras or terse aphorisms, has been the source-book and foundation of Raja Yoga. As already stated, Patanjali defines yoga as the "Chitta-vritti nirodha", or restraint of the fluctuations and modifications of the mind. In a yoga-state the mind, including intellect and ego (ahamkara) are under control and free from fluctuation, so that the mind rests in the spirit within, and consequently a jivatma is then is communion with God. Then, the state of an aspirant is like that of lamp in a windless room without any flicker. Spirit or soul is originally pure, peaceful, changeless and non-doer, but because of igorance and predominance of any of the three gunas, it begins to identify itself with body, ego, intellect or mind and suffers pleasure, pain and such other emotions. Moved and agitated by fluctuations of mind, it identifies itself with the object with which it comes in contact and experiences pain, sorrow, pleasure and joy.

ASHTANGA YOGA (EIGHT LIMBS OF YOGA)

Final release or moksha is the end, and yoga is the means. Means are as important as the end to be achieved. The means should be as noble and just as is the end and obejct in view. Raja Yoga is an invaluable aid in meditation leading to an insight into the real and original nature of the soul, which is ever pure and changeless. Raja Yoga is a depth experience, a highly developed psycho-physical technique, a practical wisdom which consists of eight stages or limbs enumerated by Patanjali as under:

1. Yama or ethical principal of self-control, are five in number. They are called ahimsa or non-injury, satya or truthfulness, asteya or non-stealing, aparigarha or non-conveting, and brahmcharya or continence.

2. Niyama or observances including saucha or purity, santosh or contentment, tapsas or austerity, svadhyaya or study of the holy scriptures, and Ishvara pranidhana or dedication and devotion to the Lord.

3. Asanas or body posture are 84 in number, but only a few of them are essential as an aid to meditation. An easy sitting posture can be chosen by the aspirant to maintain the constant and steady concentration. The most basic posture is Padmasana or the Lotus Pose. This pose symbolizes man's spiritual growth, purity and peace, and in this posture alone the rishis, gods and divinities are commonly shown meditatting.

4. Pranayama or breath control teaches how to regulate breath and thereby control the fluctuations and modification of the mind.

5. Pratyahar or withdrawal of the senses.

6. Dharana or steadying the mind by concertrating on an object for a stretch of time. The object may be the tip of your nose, the point between the eye-brow, a flowers, an idol or picture of a deity or flame of candle.

7. Dhyana or meditation is a state when a yogi's consciousness is fully absorbed in the object of meditation.

8. Samadhi or state of trance is a condition of superconsciousness, when the yogi becomes one with the object, that is, God, and his body-consciousness is completely dissolved.

The first three stages of yama, niyama and asanas are called external (bahiranga) sadhana. Yama-niyamas are the rules of conduct which help an aspirant to be in harmony with his environment and fellow-men by overcoming his passions and emotions. Various body postures and poses keep the body fit and elastic. Asanas, coupled with rhythmic and regulated breathing, make a perfect tonic for our radiant mental and physical health.

The next two stages, pranayama and pratyahara, teach how to control breath and maintain steadiness of mind, and thereby overcome the body-consciousness. Our mental activities are intimately connected with our breathing. Regulated and rhythmic breathing helps a lot in our sense-withdrawal and restraint of mental fluctuations. Many of our ills are more mental than physical. If man is mentally healthy, the body will take care of itself without much efforts. These two limbs or stages of yoga are known as internal (antaranga) sadhana.

The last three stages-dharna, dhyana and samadhi—are called the innermost (antaratma) sadhana, and lead the aspirant to the highest ideal of God or self-realization. During these final stages of spiritual growth, the mind becomes purer in essence and ultimately one with the Ishvara or Brahman, the object of contemplation and meditation. Mind is the monarch or Raja of the senses. A Raja Yogi is one who has conquered his mind, the king of the senses. Raja Yoga or the Royal Yoga teaches how to control mind and withdraw the senses from the objects of thier interest. When one has conquered his passions, emotions, thoughts and mind, he becomes a Raja yogi, a fit person to be one and united with his Creator and God. Raja Yoga aims at the sublimation and release of the spirit by balanced psycho-physical development. Body is a vehicle and an instrument, which must be brought to the level of perfection as a preparation for spiritual evolution and illumination. In the final stage of samadhi the knower, the knowledge and the known lose their separate identities and become inseparably one. This identity and unity between sadhaka, sadhana,and sadhya is the quintessence to be realized and perfected through yogic technique disciline culminating in the state of samadhi or super-consciousness.

Samadhi is the sumum bonum, the summit of the efforts and end of the long quest. It is like the dreamless state of deep sleep when there is no feeling of 'I' or 'mine'. With it the sadhaka attain the state of perfect peace, bliss, pure consciousness and rest, a state which defies description and definition, a thing to be felt and experienced and not to be described and uttered. The path to this goal is narrow, difficult and sharp like the razor's edge. The path of yoga is beset with difficulties. The storms of mental fluctuations contitue to agitate the water of mind, and then there is no mental equipoise and peace. Then there are very many hindrances and obstacles like laziness, diseases, doubts, indecision, indifference, lack of porper motivation, sensual cravings, want of continuity of efforts and score others. Keeping in view all these obstacles, our rishis have prescribed these above aids, which should be constantly used and assiduously practised. Ceaseless efforts and sadhana or practice is the key factor in the progress on the path of spirit. Spiritual sadhana is a supreme endeavour and requires utmost exertion and practice.

Between Ida and Pingla nadis flows the Sushumana nadi, the main channel of psychic energy. It runs through the spinal column. It is interescted by the two other nadis as different points, and at these points are located the six chakras (plexus) or centes of psychic energy. The lowest Chakra is called Muladhara, and is situated in the pelvic region behind the genitals. Then comes the Svadhisthana Chakra above it. Manipuraka Chakra is the third and is located at the navel; Anahata Chakra is in cardiac region; Vishuddha in pharyngeal region and Ajana Chakra is located at a point between the eyebrows. Then there is Sahashrara, the thousand-petalled lotus Chakra, at the top of the Sushumana. It is the most powerful wheel of psychic force and energy. The Ida and Pingla veins rise from the bose of the spine and terminate in the left and right nostrils. They represent the lunar and solar energies respectively.

In Muladhara wheel, the lowest centre, lies dormant the Kundalini, the "serpent power" or the celestial cosmic force. The aim and object of yogic practices is to awaken this latent psychic energy. When it is aroused and made to reach the top most Chakra of Sahasrara, piercing through all the other Chakras, a tremendous spiritual strength and energy in released within, and the yogi athains salvation. This process of awakening the 'serpent power'and making it unite in the top most wheel also results in the attainment of many supernatural powers, but they are, in fact, obstacles in the path of final release and moksha, and therefore to be escheswed and avoided.

With the awakening of this cosmic power and its union in the highest Chakra, one attains the state of super consciousness, where the 'I' and 'mine'cease to exist and God is no longer held as personal. He is then experienced as the pure Consciousness. Then all the dualities of personal and impersonal, absolute and relative, pleasure and pain, immanence and transcendence cease, and one becomes united with the Supreme Being.

DIAMOND POCKET BOOKS PRESENTS

OSHO BOOKS

Sufis : Singing Silence
Sufis : A Lotus of Emptiness
Sufis : The Glory of Freedom
Sufis : The Royal Way
I am the Gate
The Great Challenge
Meditation - the Art of Ecstasy
I say unto You-I & II
Zen and the Art of Living
Zen and the Art of Enlightenment
Zen : Take it Easy
Zen and The Art of Meditation
The Psychology of the Esoteric
The Divine Melody
A Cup of Tea
And the Flowers Showered
The Mystery Beyond Mind
The Forgotten Language
of the Heart
Towards the Unknown
Bauls : The Dancing Mystics
Bauls : The Seekers of the Path
Bauls :
The Mystics of Celebration
Bauls : The Singing Mystics
Ecstasy :
The Language of Existence
Be Oceanic
The Greatest Gamble
Vedanta : The Ultimate Truth
Vedanta :
The First Star in the Evening
Vedanta : An Art of Dying

A Taste of the Divine
One Earth One Humanity
Love & Meditation
Freedom form the mind
Life, A song, A Dance
Meeting the Ultimate
The Master is a Mirror
The Forgotten Language
of the Heart
The Alchemy of Enlightenment
From Ignorance to Innocence
Be Silent & Know
Tantra Vision :
The Secret of the Inner Experience
Tantra Vision : The Door to Nirvana
Tantra Vision :
Beyond the Barriers Wisdom
Eternal Celebration
A Song Without Words
Inner Harmony
Sing, Dance, Rejoice
Secret of Disciplehood
Laughter is My Message
The Centre of the Cyclone
Meditation : The Ultimate Adventure
New Vision for the New Millennium
Allah To Zen
Yoga : The Alpha & The Omega
The Birth of Being
Cession of Mind
The Ever-Present Flower
From Chaos to Cosmos

DIAMOND POCKET BOOKS (P) LTD.
X-30, Okhla Industrial Area, Phase-II, New Delhi-20
Ph. : (011) 6841033, 6822803, 6822804   Fax : (011) 6925020
Email : mverma@nde.vsnl.net.in

ASTROLOGY AND WEALTH
(Jyotish Aur Dhan Yoga)
Dr. Bhojraj Dwivedi

Money is the basic requirement of life but some people are not so lucky in this regard. There are various factors that do not let a person earn money but as he is unaware of adverse impact of planets, he is unable to take remedial steps. Paucity of money leads a person in dire straits. This is a unique book on the subject which fully guides a needy and poor person to own wealth by restoring to performance of certain methods. Not only this much, but the book also suggests certain methods by which a rich person can become richer. In short both the haves and have-nots can benefit equally from author's suggestions.
Price : 75/-

ASTROLOGY AND DISEASES (JYOTISH AUR ROG VICHAR)
Dr. Bhojraj Dwivedi

Most of the diseases that inflict majority of persons are caused by infavourable stars and the damaging impact cast by them. An experienced astrologer can foretell as to which of the diseases are likely to impact a native and the remedial steps requested to be taken because forewarmed is forewarmed. This book suggests ways and methods which when adopted, can reduce or do away with severity of diseases, thus ensuring a disease free state. The suggestions will also help to cut down your medical expenses.
Price : 150/-

MYSTICAL WORLD OF PALMISTRY
Dr. Bhojraj Dwivedi

What you wanted to know about palmistry and what is not found elsewhere will be found in the book which is unique, incompatible and invaluable. All the intricate and so for unknown aspects about astrology have been laid open. In a way it is the only book that explains, in details, various facets of palmistry about which only a handful of persons know. There are 600 diagrams also which succiently explain the hidden secrets of this science apart from original hand prints.
Price : 200/-

DIAMOND POCKET BOOKS PRESENTS

RELIGION & SPIRITUALITY

Mahabharata	Dr. B. R. Kishore
Ramayana	Dr. B. R. Kishore
Rigveda	Dr. B. R. Kishore
Samveda	Dr. B. R. Kishore
Yajurveda	Dr. B. R. Kishore
Atharvveda	Dr. B. R. Kishore
Hinduism	Dr. B. R. Kishore
Gods & Godesses of India	B. K. Chaturvedi
Supreme Mother Durga (Durga Chalisa)	B. K. Chaturvedi
The Hymns & Orisons of Lord Shiva (Roman)	B. K. Chaturvedi
Sri Hanuman Chalisa (Roman)	B. K. Chaturvedi
Pilgrimage Centres of India	B. K. Chaturvedi
Fast & Festivals of India	Manish Verma
Chalisa Sangrah (Roman)	R. P. Hingorani
Srimad Bhagwath Geeta (Sanskrit & English)	Dayanand Verma
Sri-Ram-Charit manas (Translated By)	S. P. Ojha
Realm of Sadhana (What Saints & Masters Say)	Chakor Ajgaonkar
Mathura & Vrindavan the Mystices Land of Lord Krishna	F. S. Growse
Saints & Mystics of India	Dr. Giriraj Shah
Saints & Gurus of India	Dr. Giriraj Shah
Glory of Indian Culture	Dr. Giriraj Shah

SAI LITERATURE

The Immortal Fakir of Shirdi	Dr. S. P. Ruhela
Sai Grace and Recent Predictions	Dr. S. P. Ruhela
The Divine Glory of Shri Shirdi Sai Baba	Dr. S. P. Ruhela
(Experiences of Devotees in the Post-Samadhi Period (1918-1997)	
Shirdi Sai : The Supreme	Dr. S. P. Ruhela
Divine Grace of Sri Shirdi Sai Baba	Dr. S. P. Ruhela
Divine Revelations of a Sai Devotee	Dr. S. P. Ruhela
Communication from the Spirit of Shri Shirdi Sai Baba	Dr. S. P. Ruhela
Sri Shirdi Sai Bhajanavali (In Roman)	Dr. S. P. Ruhela
Worship of Sri Sathya Sai Baba (In Roman)	Dr. S. P. Ruhela
His Mystery and Experiencing His Love	Dr. S. P. Ruhela
World Peace and Sri Sathya Sai Avtar	Dr. S. P. Ruhela
How to Receive Sri Sathya Sai Baba's Grace	Dr. S. P. Ruhela
Fragrant Spiritual Memories of A Karma Yogi	Dr. S. P. Ruhela
The Divine Glory of Sri Shirdi Sai Baba	Chakor Ajgaonkar
The Footprints of Shirdi Sai	Chakor Ajgaonkar
Tales from Sai Baba's Life	Chakor Ajgaonkar
Sri Shirdi Sai Baba	B. Umamaheswara Rao
Thus Spake Sri Shirdi Sai Baba	U. Umamaheswara Rao
The Spiritual Philosophy of Shri Shirdi Sai Baba Shirdi	B. Umamashwara Rao
Sai Baba of Shirdi	B. K. Chaturvedi
Sri Sathya Sai Baba : A Biography	B. K. Chaturvedi
The Miracle Man : Sri Sathya Sai Baba	B. K. Chaturvedi
The Eternal Sai	B. Manney
Sri Sathya Sai Baba : Understanding	
Rishi Ram Ram	Yogi M. K. Spencer
Oneness with God	Yogi M. K. Spencer
Quiet Talks with the Master	Eva Bell Barber
Adventures with evil Spirits	Joseph J. Ghosh
A Child from the Spirit World Speaks	K. H. Nagrani
Future is in Our Hands	A. Somasundaram